Pennsylvania Deitsh
Dictionary

A dictionary for the language
spoken by the Amish
and used in the
Pennsylvania Deitsh
New Testament

Deitsh to English
English to Deitsh

Thomas Beachy

Second Printing	August 2001
Third Printing	May 2004
Fourth Printing	August 2007
Fifth Printing	November 2010

Pennsylvania Deitsh Dictionary
ISBN 1-890050-37-7

2673 TR 421
Sugarcreek, OH 44681

Carlisle Press
WALNUT CREEK

ACKNOWLEDGMENTS

This book is dedicated to my parents, who taught me Pennsylvania Deitsh as my mother tongue. Their assistance with definitions in this dictionary was appreciated.

I wish to thank Hank Hershberger for providing direction and guidance in producing this dictionary and for editing all materials.

I thank Pablo Valencia for structuring both the Grammar and the Dictionary, and for editing all material for clarity and conciseness.

INTRODUCTION

This dictionary was written at the request of Hank Hershberger, who translated most of the New Testament into Pennsylvania Deitsh as spoken in Holmes Co., Ohio. The Dictionary, from Deitsh to English, is meant to accompany *Es Nei Teshtament*. Consequently, the words listed in it consist of the vocabulary used in *Es Nei Teshtament*, and their definitions in English reflect the Holmes Co., Ohio, usage. The spelling of the words is also the same as that used in *Es Nei Teshtament* and the primer: *Ich Kann Pennsylvania Deitsh Laysa* with some exceptions.

The section "Basics of Deitsh Grammar" found at the front of the Dictionary is meant to help the reader understand word relationships and word families in Pennsylvania Deitsh, so that their "Dictionary form" is understood and can be found easily in the Dictionary. For example, it is advisable for persons interested in *Es Nei Teshtament* who are not thoroughly familiar with the verb forms of Pennsylvania Deitsh, to read such information in the "Basics of Deitsh Grammar" before attempting to look up unfamiliar verb forms in the Dictionary. For instance, "bisht" is not found in the dictionary, but its infinitive form, "sei," is.

The "Basics of Deitsh Grammar" is not meant to be exhaustive, and it gives only such information as may be found useful for the user of the Dictionary. It is hoped that this section is succinct and clear so that both, native speakers of Pennsylvania Deitsh, and of English, can benefit from its explanations when using the Dictionary.

The user of the Dictionary should be aware of the "Chart of Abbreviations and Symbols" and refer to it as needed when looking up words in the Dictionary. Since Pennsylvania Deitsh is not widely written, it has not been codified to general satisfaction, and a great amount of free variation is present in spelling and usage. Some spellings have been accepted since the first printing of *Es Nei Teshtament*, and these spellings appear in the Dictionary. The changes are minor and the user of the Dictionary will spot them easily. (Ex. *-ung* endings are now accepted as *-ing*) The "Chart" will be helpful to understand particular forms and usages of given words listed in the Dictionary.

CONTENTS

ABBREVIATIONS and SYMBOLS

Abbreviations used in the Deitsh to English Dictionary

(f)   feminine

(form)   formal use only

(iv)   irregular verb – so indicated after its past participle
          (Cf. Irregu-lar Verb Chart, p. XXI)

(lit)   literal meaning

(m)   masculine

(neu)   neuter

(pl)   plural

(pref)   prefix

(ss)   verb with special stem (Cf. Grammar Section below, Special
          Verbal Stems, p. XVIII)

Past participles of all verbs are given in parenthesis after the infinitive:

abbrecha   (abgebrocha)   to break off

*an asterisk after the past participle indicates that the past of this verb is formed with the verb sei as an auxiliary (cf. Grammar Section below, Past Tense of Verbs p. XIX)

gay (ganga)*   to go

Further abbreviations used in the English to Deitsh Dictionary

(n)   noun
(v)   verb
(adj)   adjective
(adv)   adverb

BASICS of DEITSH GRAMMAR

Gender

All Deitsh nouns have one of three genders: masculine, feminine and neuter. The gender of nouns causes gender to be shown in the following word classes:

> definite articles
> adjectives
> adverbs (when modifying adjectives)
> past participles (when functioning as adjectives)

Definite Article

Masculine	Feminine	*Neuter*
da (**da** mann)	**di** (**di** fraw)	**es** (**es** kind)
the man	*the woman*	*the child*

The dative case of the definite article is **em**. Em is only used with masculine and neuter nouns.

Ich gebb **em** mann en buch.   *I give a book to the man.*

The plural definite article for all genders is **di**.

Contraction 's

The contraction **'s** may represent the definite article **es** or the pronoun **es** (often representing the impersonal *it* as in *It* is cold today). Both representations are usually attached to a preposition or the verb **sei**.

in**'s** haus   *in the house*
'sis kald heit   *It is cold today.*

Indefinite Article

Deitsh has only one indefinite article, **en**.

en mann   *a man*
en abbel   *an apple*

Diminutives

Diminutives of nouns (often expressing endearment) can be formed with the suffix **-li** (plural **-len**) which turns the noun into neuter. Many nouns are changed into diminutives through internal changes. Diminutives are easily recognizable and are not listed separately in the dictionary.

da haws	*the rabbit*
es haws**li**	*the little rabbit*
di haws**len**	*the little rabbits*

Adjectives

When adjectives are preceded by the indefinite article, they show gender by adding the appropriate suffix. N.B. No suffix is added to neuter adjectives.

Masculine	Feminine	Neuter
-ah (en grohs**ah** mann)	-i (en grohs**i** fraw)	**0** (en grohs kind)
a big man	*a big woman*	*a big child*

Adjectives appear in the dictionary in their neuter form.

Comparative and Superlative of Adjectives

The suffixes **-ah** and **-sht** are added to adjectives to form the comparative and superlative of adjectives.

dikk	dikk**ah**	dik**sht**
thick	*thicker*	*thickest*

Only irregular comparatives and superlatives are listed in the dictionary.

Adjectives can be changed to pronouns by adding one of the following three endings.

-ah (masculine)

Sellah gaul is goot.	*That horse is good.*
Sell is en good**ah**.	*That is a good one (referring to horse).*

-i (feminine)

Sell is en goodi shtoahri.	*That is a good story.*
Sell is en good**i**.	*That is a good one (referring to story).*

-es (neuter)

Sell is en goot buch.	*That is a good book.*
Sell is en good**es**.	*That is a good one (referring to book).*

Dative Form of Adjectives

Only adjectives modifying masculine and neuter nouns show the dative ending by adding the suffix -a.

zu em grohs**a** mann	*to the big man*
zu em grohs**a** kind	*to the big child*

Adjectival Past Participles

Past participles show gender when they are used as adjectives. Their suffixes are the same as those of adjectives.

en fashtaund**ah** mann	en fashtaund**i fraw**	en fashtaund kind
a surprised man	*a surprised woman*	*a surprised child*

Changing Adjectives to Nouns

Some (not all) adjectives can be changed to nouns by adding the suffix **-hayt**, **-heit** or **-keit**. Adjectives of this type are listed in the Dictionary, with the appropriate suffix, when they appear in *Es Nei Teshtament*.

dankboah	thankful
dankboahkeit (f)	thankfulness
folkumma	perfect
folkummaheit (f)	perfection
ksund	healthy
ksundhayt (f)	health

XIV

Adverbs

Adverbs show gender when modifying adjectives. The suffixes are the same as those of adjectives.

Masculine	Feminine	Neuter
en adlich**ah** grohsah mann	en adlich**i grohsi** fraw	en adlich grohs kind
a fairly big man	*a fairly big woman*	*a fairly big child*

Verbs

Verbs have different endings to agree with the subject in person and number. Regular verbs are conjugated as shown in the chart below.

	lawfa	*to walk*
ich	lawf	*I walk*
du	lawf-sht	*you (singular) walk*
eah/see/es	lawf-**t**	*he/she/it walks*
miah	lawf-**a**	*we walk*
diah	lawf-**et**	*you (plural) walk*
si	lawf-**a**	*they walk*

N.B. a) The endings reflect the person and number of the subject (the first person singular is indicated by not showing any particular ending).

b) The we- and they- forms of the verbs are normally the same as the infinitive.

Verbs with Separable Prefix

Some verbs have separable prefixes. They are conjugated as shown in the chart below.

ausfinna	*to find out*
ich finn sell **aus**	*I find that out*
du finsht sell **aus**	*you find that out*
eah/see/es find sell **aus**	*he/she/it finds that out*
miah finna sell **aus**	*we find that out*
diah finnet sell **aus**	*you find that out*
si finna sell **aus**	*they find that out*

But: Ich vill sell **ausfinna**.	*I want to find that out.*

Verb prefix ge-

Many Deitsh verbs can take the prefix **ge-** (not to be confused with the past participle) to form a verbal noun. The prefix **ge-** adds one or both of the following meanings to the verb:

a) habitual action	Sei **ge**shvetz macht mich meet.
	His (habitual) talking makes me tired.
b) action "of some peculiar kind"	Ich binn sei **ge**shvetz laydich.
	I'm tired of his (peculiar kind of) talk.

The verb suffix -es

Most verbs can take the suffix **-es** to form a verbal noun.

Shpring**es** macht em meet.   *Running makes one tired.*

The infinitive may be frequently used in the same way.

Shpring**a** macht em meet.   *Running (to run) makes one tired.*

Verb suffix -ah

The suffix **-ah** added to a verbal stem carries the meaning *one who* (comparable to the English suffix *-er*).

Eah is en shpring**ah**.   *He is a runner.*

The pronunciation of this suffix contrasts with that of the infinitive ending **-a**:

Eah is am shpring**a**.   *He is running.*

Irregular verbs

Conjugations of irregular verbs are listed in a separate chart on p. XXI, and are indicated by (iv) in the dictionary after their past participle.

XVII

Special Verbal Stems

Some verb conjugations, while not irregular in their endings, show changes in the verbal stems to which the endings are attached.

veahra *to wear*		**sawwa** *to say*	
veah	veah**ra**	saw**k**	saw**wa**
veahsht	veah**ret**	saw**k**sht	saw**wet**
veaht	veah**ra**	saw**kt**	saw**wa**

fleeya *to fly*		**hayva** *to hold*	
flee**k**	flee**ya**	hay**b**	hay**va**
flee**k**sht	flee**yet**	hay**b**sht	hay**vet**
flee**kt**	flee**ya**	hay**bt**	hay**va**

Verbs with special stems are indicated in the dictionary by (ss) after their past participle.

Past Tense of Verbs

The past participle form of the verb, which appears in the dictionary in parenthesis alongside the infinitive, is used in Deitsh to express a past tense, in combination with the appropriate form of **havva** or **sei**. Most verbs use a form of **havva** as an auxiliary verb.

Ich shaff	*I work*
Ich **habb** kshaft	*I worked (I have worked)*

Some verbs use a form of **sei** as an auxiliary, and these are indicated in the dictionary by an asterisk after the past participle (Cf. Chart of Abbreviations and Symbols, p. IX).

Example: Ich gay	*I go*
Ich **binn** ganga	*I went (I have gone)*

Verbs that use both havva *and* sei

Same as some English verbs, many Deitsh verbs may be used in two types of constructions:

a) in active voice constructions where the subject is the doer of the action:

Da hund **hott** da mann **gebissa**.	*The dog bit the man.*

b) in passive voice constructions where the subject is the receiver of the action:

Da hund **is gebissa vadda**.	*The dog got bitten.*

In Deitsh, such verbs adopt a form of the verb **havva** as an auxiliary to form the past when used in the active voice, and adopt a form of the verb **sei** (usually accompanied by **vadda** = become) when used in the passive voice.

Changing Verbs to Adjectives

Some (not all) verbs can be changed to adjectives by adding the suffixes
-ich or **-ish**.

glawva (geglawbt)	*to believe*
glawvich	*believing, having faith*
fagunna (fagunna)	*1. to envy; 2. to desire another's misfortune*
fagunnish	*1. envious; 2. malicious*

Irregular Verbs

These verbs are not regular. Their full conjugations are shown on the following chart. Note that some of these verbs can have separable prefixes (Cf. Verbs with separable prefixes, p. XVI).

du		**sei**	
du	doon	binn	sinn
dusht	doond	bisht	sind
dutt	doon	is	sinn

gay		**shtay**	
gay	gayn	shtay	shtayn
gaysht	gaynd	shtaysht	shtaynd
gayt	gayn	shtayt	shtayn

greeya		**vella**	
grikk	greeya	vill	vella
griksht	greeyet	vitt	vellet
grikt	greeya	vill	vella

havva		**voahra**	
habb	henn	voaht	voahra
hosht	hend	voahtsht	voahret
hott	henn	voaht	voahra

Irregular verbs with separable prefixes:

ausgay	**fagay**	**foahgay**	**ohdu**
eigay	**fashtay**	**foahvissa**	

PRONUNCIATION GUIDE

Vowels

Short Vowels

a	like English **a** in wh**a**t, e.g. h**a**tt "*hard*"
ae	like English **a** in r**a**t, e.g. d**ae**tt "*dad/father*"
e	like English **e** in g**e**t, e.g. v**e**sh "*to wash*"
i	like English **i** in f**i**t, e.g. d**i**kk "*thick*"
o	like German **o** in G**o**tt, e.g. k**o**bb "*head*"
u	like English **u** in p**u**t, e.g. d**u**tt "*does*"

Long Vowels

aw	like English **aw** in th**aw**, e.g. n**aw**s "*nose*"
ay	like English **ay** in s**ay**, e.g. m**ay**t "*girls*"
ee	like English **ee** in f**ee**t, e.g. f**ee**s "*feet*"
oh	like German **oh** in **oh**r, e.g. **oh**vet "*evening*"
oo	like English **oo** in m**oo**n, e.g. h**oo**t "*hat*"

Vowel Glides

au	like English **ou** in ho**u**se, e.g. g**au**l *"horse"*
ei	like English **ei** in h**ei**ght, e.g. h**ei**t *"today"*
oi	like English **oy** in b**oy**, e.g. h**oi** *"hay"*
eah	Not in English or German, e.g. g**eah**n *"gladly"*
uah	Not in English or German, e.g. f**uah** *"team"*
iah	Not in English or German, e.g. d**iah** *"animal/you (plural)"*
oah	Not in English or German, e.g. **oah** *"ear"*

Important: The **ah** in the last four glides above replaces the standard German **r**. See **r** below.

Consonants

In most instances consonants are pronounced as they are in German and/or English. Only those consonants which are not similar in both languages are listed below.

ch	like German **ch** in ma**ch**t, e.g. i**ch** *"I"*
r	The **r** sound is written only when it is pronounced, e.g. **r**und *"round."* The traditional German **r** is usually pronounced as **a** or **ah** and is written as such. German words like:

> hart *"hard"*   hafer *"oats"*   fuhr *"team"*
>
> gern *"gladly"*   tier *"animal"*   ohr *"ear"*

then become Pennsylvania Deitsh:

> hatt, havvah, fuah, geahn, diah, and oah,

respectively.

v	like English **v** in **v**ote, e.g. **v**assah *"water"*
	Note: **v** is never pronounced as English **f**.

w   used in the long vowel **aw**, e.g. ha**w**s *"rabbit"*
Note: **w** is never pronounced as English **v**.

x   like English **x** in fo**x**, e.g. ni**x** *"nothing"*

y   like English **y** in **y**oung, e.g. **y**oah *"year"*
also used in long vowel **ay**, e.g. na**y** *"no"*

z   like English **ts** in roo**ts**, but occurs word initially only, e.g. **z**u *"to"*

tz   like English **ts** in roo**ts**, but occurs word medially and finally only, e.g. bu**tz**a *"to clean,"* hi**tz** *"heat"*

Accents

'   stress/accent is marked on the syllable which receives the primary accent.

`   secondary accent is marked when essential.
Note: The stress/accent is already marked throughout the Bible as part of the normal spelling of the word when it occurs between vowels, e.g. fa'achta *"to ignore"*

Free Variation

Some Deitsh words have variant pronunciations and spellings with no changes in meaning. They are listed with a slash as follows:

eahn/-d (f)	harvest; eahnda (pl)
gnawdi/gnawt (f)	grace
gnawt/gnawdi (f)	grace

Deitsh to English

A

ab	1. off; 2. (pref) off; 3. strange
'ab`bild (neu)	image; abbildah (pl)
'ab`brecha	to break off
'ab`dekka (abgedekt)	to uncover
'ab`fall (m)	apostasy
'ab`geddah-`deensht (m)	idol worship; abgeddah-deenshta (pl)
'ab`geddahrei (neu)	idolatry; abgeddahreiya (pl)
'ab`geddish	idolatrous
'ab`gott (m)	idol; abgeddah (pl)
'ab`gott-`deenah (m)	worshipper of idols; abgott-deenah (pl)
'ab`gott-`gleichnis (neu)	likeness of an idol; abgott-gleichnissa (pl)
'ab`hakka (abkakt)	to chop off
'ab`heicha (abkeicht)	to listen
'ab`keela (abgekeeld)	to cool off
'ab`layya (abglaykt) (ss)	to lay off
'ab`nemma (abgnumma)	to take off
a`boahma (aboahmd)	to show mercy
'ab`shidla (abkshiddeld)	to shake off
'ab`shneida (abkshnidda)	to cut off
'ab`shreiva (abkshrivva) (ss)	1. to write off; 2. to copy
'ab`shteahra (abkshteaht) (ss)	to start off
'ab`voahra (abgvoaht) (ss)	to serve
acht	eight
'achta (gacht)	to heed
'acht`zay	eighteen
'achtzich	eighty
'adda	or
'addah (m)	command; addahs (pl)

2

'adlich	pretty much, fairly
'adning (f)	1. set of church standards; adninga (pl); 2. orderliness
ah	he, unstressed form of "eah"
'akkah (m)	acre; akkah (pl)
a`langa (alangt)	to attain
'alla`veil	presently
a`lawbnis (f)	permission, allowance; alawbnissa (pl)
a`lawva (alawbt) (ss)	to allow
ald	old; eldah, eldsht
'ald`vannish	indifferent
'allem	1. all; 2."allem nohch," idiomatic construction meaning apparently
'alles	everything
'alli	every
'alli-`haychsht	highest of all
'Alli-`Haychsht (m)	the Highest (God)
'alli-`heilichsht	holiest of all
'Alli-`Heilichsht (m)	the Holiest (God)
al`mechtich	almighty
'al`mohsa (f)	alms; almohsa (pl)
als	oftentimes, at one time, at times
'alsa`mohl	sometimes
'alsnoch	yet, still
am	1.+ infinitive, expresses action in progress: "si sinn am shaffa" (They are working); 2. at the, contraction of "an em"
'amma	contraction of "am en"
a`mohl	at once (always preceded by "uf")
an	at

3

'an`dem	probably
'and`vadda (gandvat)	to answer
angsht (m)	anxiety; engshta (pl)
'anna	1. at, there; 2. (pref) at, there
'annah	other
'annahshtah	otherwise
'anres	another one; anrah (m); anri (f), (pl)
a`poshtel (m)	apostle; aposhtla (pl)
a`poshtel-`deensht (m)	office of the apostle; aposhtel-deenshta (pl)
aus	1. out of; 2. extinguished; 3. (pref) out
'ausa	outside of
'ausah	outside
'ausahlich	pertaining to that which is outward and visible
'ausahri	1. outer; 2. outside ones, non-native
'ausahsht	outermost
'aus`brecha (ausgebrocha)	to break out (sickness)
'aus`broviahra (ausbroviaht) (ss)	1. to try out; 2. to irritate, annoy
'aus`dayla (ausgedayld)	to deal or portion out
'aus`drawwa (ausgedrawwa) (ss)	1. to carry out an undertaking; 2. to define
'aus`drayya (ausgedrayt)	to turn out
'aus`dredda (ausgedredda)	1. to tread out; 2. to step aside
'aus`dreiva (ausgedrivva) (ss)	to drive out, expel
'aus`eeva (ausgeebt) (ss)	to take revenge
'aus`eeves (neu)	revenge taking
'aus`eevish	revengeful
'aus`fiahra (auskfiaht) (ss)	to enact, carry out
'aus`finna (auskfunna)	to find out
'aus`fix	upset, out of fix

4

'aus`frohwa (auskfrohkt) (ss)	to inquire about
'aus`gay (ausganga)* (iv)	1. to become extinguished (light or fire); 2. to terminate (meetings)
'aus`gevva (ausgevva) (ss)	1. to distribute; 2. to give out or expire
'aus`gevvah (m)	one who gives or passes out; ausgevvah (pl)
'aus`gnumma	except, unless
'aus`grawva (ausgegrawva) (ss)	to dig out
'aus`gukka (ausgegukt)	1. to look out for; 2. to examine
'aus`halda (auskalda)	to hold out, endure
'aus`hayva (auskohva) (ss)	to hold out
'aus`keahra (ausgekeaht) (ss)	to sweep out
'aus`layying (f)	definition; auslayyinga (pl)
'aus`layya (ausglaykt) (ss)	to define
'aus`layyah (m)	expositor; auslayyah (pl)
'aus`leahra (ausgleaht) (ss)	to pour out
'aus`lendah (m)	foreigner; auslendah (pl)
'aus`macha (ausgmacht)	1. to decide; 2. to extinguish a light or fire; 3. to matter; 4. to fare; 5. in gardening – to dig out vegetables
'aus`messa (ausgmessa)	to measure out
'aus`nannah	spread out, scattered
'aus`nemma (ausgnumma)	1. to take revenge; 2. to remove the entrails of, to gut; 3. to remove (clothes)
'aus`redda (ausgret)	to excuse
'aus`reisa (ausgrissa)	to tear out
'aus`reiva (ausgrivva) (ss)	to rub out
'aus`ret (f)	excuse; ausredda (pl)
'aus`richta (ausgricht)	to set a matter straight
'aus`roofa (ausgroofa)	1. to call out; 2. to publish a couple for marriage

5

'aus`satz (m)	leprosy
'aus`setzich	leprous
'aus`shaffa (auskshaft)	to work out
'aus`shidla (auskshiddeld)	to shake out
'aus`veahra (ausgvoahra) (ss)	to wear out
'aus`vendich	outward, on the outside
'aus`vennich	memorized, by heart
'aut`seidah (m)	outsider; autseidahs (pl)
'aut`seit	outside
a`vayla (avayld)	to choose
a`vayling (f)	choice; avaylinga (pl)
'avvah	1. but; 2. particle placed in front of adjectives to add emphasis; 3. too – used to contradict
aw	also
'awdlah (m)	eagle; awdlah (pl)
awk (neu)	eye; awwa (pl)
awl	all
'awldah (m)	altar; awldahra (pl)
awl`mechtich	almighty
'awwa-`blikk (m)	blink of an eye; awwa-blikk (pl)
'awwa-`shmiah (f)	eye salve; awwa-shmiahra (pl)
'awwa-`vassah (neu)	tears
ax	1. ax; 2. axle; ex (pl)
ay	one
'ay`brecha (aygebrocha)	to commit adultery
'ay`brechah (m)	one who commits adultery; aybrechah (pl)
'ay`bruch (neu)	adultery; aybrucha (pl)
'Ay`faw	Eve
'ay`feldich	having the affections set on one person or object

6

'aykna/ ayya	one`s own
'aykna (gaykend)	1. to own; 2. to owe
ayl (neu)	oil; ayla (pl)
'ayl-`berg (m)	Mount of Olives; ayl-berga (pl)
'ayl-`bohm (m)	olive tree; ayl-baym (pl)
'ayl-`frucht (neu)	olive berries; ayl-frichta (pl)
aym	one
'aymah (m)	pail; aymahra (pl)
ayn	one
aynd	one of several
'aynich	agreed
'aynichkeit (f)	unity; aynichkeida (pl)
'aynra	one
ayns	one
'aynsisht	only
'aysel (m)	donkey; aysela (pl)
'aysel-hutsh (m)	donkey colt; aysel-hutsha (pl)
'ayva	level, flat; ayvenah; ayvesht
'ayvich	eternal
'ayvichkeit (f)	eternity; ayvichkeida (pl)
'ayvichlich	eternally
'ayya/aykna	one`s own

B

ba`biah (neu)	paper; babiahra (pl)
'badda (gebatt)	to aid or benefit
'baddah (m)	bother; baddahra (pl)
'badra (gebaddaht)	to bother
'bakka (gebakka)	to bake
'bakka (m)	cheek; bakka (pl)
'balka (m)	wooden beam; balka (pl)
ball	1. nearly; 2. soon

PENNSYLVANIA DEITSH DICTIONARY

bam`hatzich	merciful
bam`hatzichkeit (f)	mercifulness; bamhatzichkeida (pl)
band (m)	1. ring; 2. collar; 3. fetter; banda (pl)
bang	worried
bank (f)	bench; benk (pl)
basht (f)	husk; bashta (pl)
bauch (m)	stomach; beich (pl)
baut	nearly
'bauwa (gebaut) (ss)	to build
'bavvah (m)	farmer; bavvah (pl)
'bavvah`rei (f)	farm; bavvahreiya (pl)
bay (neu)	leg; bay (pl)
'bayda (gebayda)	to pray
bays	angry
'baysa (m)	broom; baysa (pl)
'bayt-`box (f)	phylactery (lit. prayer box); bayt-boxa (pl)
'bayt-`haus (neu)	house of prayer; bayt-heisah (pl)
beah (m)	bear; beahra (pl)
'bedla (gebeddeld)	to beg
be`dreebt	grieved
be`drohwa	betrayed
'beebli (neu)	chick; beeblen (pl)
'beeda (gebodda)	1. to offer; 2. to win; 3. to bid
'beeya (gebohwa)	to bend
be`graybnis (neu)	grave; begraybnissa (pl)
be`greifa (begriffa)	to comprehend
bei	by
'beisa (gebissa)	to bite
be`kand	familiar
be`keahra (bekeaht)	to repent
be`kendnis (neu)	confession; bekendnissa (pl)

8

be`kenna (bekend)	to confess
be`kimmahra (bekimmaht)	to take concern about
be`leebt	beloved
bell (f)	bell; bella (pl)
belt (neu)	belt; beldah (pl)
'bendel (m)	string; bendla (pl)
berg (m)	mountain; berga (pl)
be`roof (m)	calling, office; beroofa (pl)
be`shneida (beshnidda)	to circumcise
be`shneiding (f)	circumcision; beshneidinga (pl)
besht	best
'beshta	the best
be`shveahra (beshvoahra)	to exorcise
be`shveahrah (m)	exorcist
'bessah	better
'bessahs	a better thing
bett (neu)	bed; beddah (pl)
be`vaykt	moved
be`zawla (bezawld)	to pay
be`zawling (f)	payment; bezawlinga (pl)
'bichli (neu)	small book; bichlen (pl)
'bidda (gebitt)	to ask for, request
'bidda (gebodda)	to bid (peace, greeting etc.)
'biddah	bitter
'biddah`greidah (pl)	bitter herbs (wormwood)
'biddahlich	bitterly
'bikka (gebikt)	1. to stoop; 2. to bow
bild (neu)	image; bildah (pl)
bill (neu)	invoice; bills (pl)
'binna (gebunna)	to tie
'bishof (m)	bishop; bishofs (pl)
'bisli	a little

9

biss	until
'bissel	a little
'blakka (m)	spot; blekka (pl)
blank (f)	plank; blanka (pl)
'blansa (f)	plant; blansa (pl)
'blansa (geblanst)	to plant
blatt (f)	leaf; bleddah (pl)
blatz (m)	1. place; 2. space; bletz (pl)
'blayyich	pale
'bleiva (geblivva)* (ss)	to remain or stay
ble`siah (m)	pleasure; blesiahra (pl)
'bletzlich	immediately
blind	blind
'blind`heit (f)	blindness; blindheida (pl)
'blitza (geblitzt)	to flash
bloh	blue
blohk (m)	1. plague; 2. bother; blohwa (pl)
'blohk-`frei	free from disturbance
'blohsa (geblohsa)	to blow
'blohsah (m)	blower; blohsah (pl)
'blohs-`hann (f)	horn; blohs-hanna (pl)
'blohwa (geblohkt) (ss)	to bother
'blohwich	bothersome
'blooda (geblooda)	to bleed
blook (m)	plow; bloowa (pl)
bloot (neu)	blood
'bloot-`feld (neu)	field of blood; bloot-feldah (pl)
'bloots-`drobba (m)	drop of blood; bloots-drobba (pl)
'bloots-`granket (f)	bleeding sickness; bloots-grankeda (pl)
'bloot-`shtrayma (m)	bloodstream; bloot-shtrayma (pl)
'bloowa (geblookt) (ss)	to plow

blumm (f)	flower; blumma (pl)
blutt	naked
boat (neu)	boat; boats (pl)
'bobli (neu)	baby; boblen (pl)
'bodda (m)	ground, floor; bodda (pl)
'bodda-`nesht (neu)	blankets put on floor for bed; bodda-neshtah (pl)
'boddel (f)	bottle; bodla (pl)
bohm (m)	tree; baym (pl)
boo (m)	boy; boova (pl)
boos (f)	repentance
'boovli (neu)	little boy; boovlen (pl)
'bot`shaftah (m)	ambassador; botshaftah (pl)
bow (f)	bow; bows (pl)
bowl (f)	bowl; bowls (pl)
box (f)	box; boxa (pl)
'braekka (gebraekt)	to brag
'brand-`opfah (neu)	burnt offering; brand-opfahra (pl)
brass	brass
'braucha (gebraucht)	1. to need; 2. to perform magical healing arts (powwow)
'brayding (f)	width; brayding (pl)
brayt	wide
'brecha (gebrocha)	to break
'breddich (f)	sermon; breddicha (pl)
'breddicha (gebreddicht)	to preach
'breddichah (m)	preacher; breddichah (pl)
'breddiches (neu)	preaching
'breedahlich	brotherly
breef (m)	letter (postal); breefa (pl)
'breichta (gebreicht)	would need
'brenna (gebrend)	to burn

11

'brilla (gebrild)	to cry
'brilles (neu)	crying
'bringa (gebrocht)	to bring
bro`fayda-`vadda (pl)	prophecy, words of the prophets
bro`fayda-`veib (neu)	prophetess; brofayda-veivah (pl)
bro`fayt (m)	prophet; brofayda (pl)
broffet`zeiya (gebroffetzeit) (ss)	to prophesy
broffet`zeiya-`vadda (pl)	words of prophecy
broffet`zeiying (f)	prophecy; broffetzeiyinga (pl)
broht (neu)	bread
'broht-`fesht (neu)	feast of bread; broht-feshta (pl)
'brokka (m)	crumb; brokka (pl)
'broodah (m)	brother; breedah (pl)
bro`viahra (broviaht) (ss)	to try
'brunna (m)	1. well; 2. fountain; brunna (pl)
brusht (f)	breast; brisht (pl)
'brusht-`playt (neu)	breastplate; brusht-playts (pl)
buch (neu)	book; bichah (pl)
'bukkel (m)	back; bikkel (pl)
bull (m)	bull; bulla (pl)
bund (m)	covenant; bunda (pl)
'bundel (m)	bundle; bundla (pl)
'bundes-`lawt (m)	ark of the covenant; bundes-lawda (pl)
'bushel (f)	bushel; bushel (pl)
'bushel-`koahb (m)	bushel basket; bushel-keahb (pl)
'bush-`feiyah (neu)	forest fire; bush-feiyahra (pl)
'bush`tawb (m)	letter of alphabet; bushtawva (pl)
'butza (gebutzt)	to clean

12

C

cent (m)	cent; cent (pl)
'Christus (m)	Christ
crowd (f)	crowd; crowds (pl)
'crystal-`glaws (neu)	crystal glass; crystal-glessah (pl)
'curtain (neu)	curtain; curtains (pl)

D

da (m)	the
'dabbah	quick
dach (neu)	roof; dechah (pl)
'dadda (gedatt/fadatt)*	to wither
'daddel-`daub (f)	turtle dove; daddel-dauva (pl)
daett (m)	father; daedda (pl)
dank (m)	thanks
'danka (gedankt)	to thank
'dankboah	thankful
'dankboahkeit (f)	thankfulness; dankboahkeida (pl)
'dankes (neu)	giving of thanks
dann	1. in that case; 2. for that reason; 3. as a consequence
dann (f)	thorn; danna (pl)
'dansa (gedanst)	to dance
dasht (m)	thirst
'dashtich	thirsty
datt	there
daub (f)	dove; dauva (pl)
'daufa (daufa)	to be allowed
'dausend (f)	thousand; dausends (pl)
'davvahra (gedavvaht) (ss)	to pity
dawb	deaf
dawf (f)	baptism; dawfa (pl)

13

'dawfa (gedawft)	to baptize
dawk	illuminated with daylight
dawk (m)	day; dawwa (pl)
dawks	in the daytime
'dawlah (m)	dollar; dawlah (pl)
dayk (m)	dough; dayka (pl)
'daykli (neu)	small dough; dayklen (pl)
dayl	some, certain ones
dayl (neu)	portion; daylah (pl)
'dayla (gedayld)	1. to share; 2. to deal or portion out
'day`meedich	humble
'day`meedicha (gedaymeedicht)	to humble oneself
'day`meedichkeit (f)	attitude of humility
'day`moot (f)	humility
dayt	would
deah (f)	door; deahra (pl)
deah (m)	1. this; 2. this one
'deah-`heedah (m)	doorkeeper; deah-heedah (pl)
deahm (f)	intestines
'deahra	this
dee (f)	this
deeb (m)	thief; deeb (pl)
deef	deep
'deefa (neu)	the deep
'deena (gedeend)	1. to worship; 2. to serve
'deenah (m)	1. servant; 2. ordained minister in a church; deenah (pl)
'deensht-`gnecht (m)	servant; deensht-gnechta (pl)
'deensht-`leit (pl)	servants
'deensht-`mawt (f)	servant maid; deensht-mawda (pl)
dei	your
deich	through

'deidlich	clear, distinct
deift	would be allowed
deim	your
dein	yours
deina	your
'deinra	your
'Deivel (m)	devil; deivela (pl)
'deivilish	devilish
'deiyah	expensive
'dekka (gedekt)	to cover
'dellah (m)	plate; dellahra (pl)
demm	this
'denka (gedenkt)	to think
'denna (pl)	those
dess (neu)	this
di (f)	the
di (pl)	the
diah	you (nominative plural)
diah (dative singular)	you
diah (neu)	animal; diahra (pl)
di`bei	present or included with
dich	you (accusative singular)
di`deich	1. because of it; 2. through it; 3. thereby
di`foah	1. before; 2. in favor of
di`freind	in relation by blood or marriage
di`funn	1. from; 2. from here
di`geyya	against, opposed
di`haym	at home
dikk	thick
'dikk-`kebbich	stubborn
dill	anise, anathon, dill

'dimla (gedimmeld)	to thunder
'Dimmels-`kinnah (pl)	children of thunder
'dinda (f)	ink
ding (neu)	thing; dingah (pl)
'dinga (gedunga)	to hire
'dinka (gedinkt)	to seem
di`nohch	1. afterward; 2. depending on, according to
di`nohvet	tonight
dish (m)	table; disha (pl)
'dishtel (m)	thistle; dishtla (pl)
di`tzu	1. to it; 2. to whom; 3. included
di`veaht	worthwhile
di`veyya	about it
di`vorce-`shreives (neu)	divorce writing; divorce-shreivinga (pl)
do	here
doah (neu)	1. gate; 2. large barn door; doahra (pl)
doch	after all, still
'dochtah (f)	daughter; dechtah (pl)
'dohdes-`engel (m)	death angel; dohdes-engla (pl)
doht	dead
'doht-`shlayyah (m)	murderer; doht-shlayyah (pl)
'doktah (m)	doctor; doktahra
'dracha-`diah (neu)	dragon; dracha-diahra (pl)
draub (f)	grape; drauva (pl)
draus	out there
'drauva-`feld (neu)	vineyard; drauva-feldah (pl)
'drauva-`goahra (m)	vineyard; drauva-goahra (pl)
'drauva-`shtokk (m)	grapevine; drauva-shtekk (pl)
'drauwa (gedraut)	1. to trust; 2. to dare
'drawwa (gedrawwa) (ss)	to carry

16

dray (f)	a turn or bend; drayya (pl)
'drayshta (gedraysht)	to comfort
'drayshtah (m)	one who comforts; drayshtah (pl)
'drayya (gedrayt)	to turn
'dredda (gedredda)	to tread
'dreeb`sawl (f)	sorrow
'dreffa (gedroffa)	to make contact with, to meet or hit
drei	three
'dreisich	thirty
'dreiva (gedrivva) (ss)	1. to drive, chase; 2. to propel physically; 3. to motivate
drekk (m)	dirt
'drekkich	dirty
'drekk-`loch (neu)	1. mud puddle; 2. muddy patch of ground; drekk-lechah (pl)
'dresha (gedrosha)	to thresh
'dresha-`floah (m)	threshing floor; dresha-floahra (pl)
'dresha-`shaufel (f)	winnowing fork; dresha-shaufla (pl)
'dridda	the third one
'driddel (neu)	a third part
'drikka (gedrikt)	to press or squeeze
'drikla (gedrikkeld)	to dry
drink (m)	a drink; drinks (pl)
'drinka (gedrunka)	to drink
'drinkes (neu)	beverage
'drink-`opfah (neu)	drink offering; drink-opfahra (pl)
drinn	in there
dritt	the third
'drivva	over there
'drivvah	across
droh	1. doing it; 2. near it; 3. fastened to it; 4. (separable prefix) about, at, concerning, of

17

drohm (m) — dream; drohma (pl)
'drohma (gedrohmd) — to dream
'drohmah (m) — dreamer
drohsht (m) — comfort, assurance
'drohshta (gedrohsht) — to comfort
'droiya (gedroit) — to threaten
'drovva — up there
drubb (f) — group; drubba (pl)
druff — on there
'drukka — dry; drukkanah, drukkesht
'drukka (gedrukt) — to print, produce type with a machine
drumm — 1. closely around it; 2. concerning it; 3. therefore
'drunna — down there
'druvvel (m) — trouble; druvla (pl)
'druvvel-`machah (m) — troublemaker; druvvel-machah (pl)
'druvla (gedruvveld) — to trouble
du — you (nominative, singular)
du (gedu) (iv) — 1. to do; 2. to put
duch (neu) — cloth; dichah (pl)
'dum`hayda (pl) — follies
'dumhaydichkeit (f) — foolishness; dumhaydichkeida (pl)
'dumla (gedummeld) — to hurry
dumm — 1. not intelligent; 2. funny
'dunka (gedunkt) — to dip
'dunkel — dark
'dunkelheit (f) — darkness; dunkelhayda (pl)

E

eah — he
eah (f) — honor, glory
'eahb`shaft (f) — inheritance; eahbshafta (pl)

'eahb`shaft-fa`daylah (m)	one who apportions an inheritance; eahbshaft-fadaylah (pl)
'eahdich	earthen
'eah`geitz (m)	selfish desire for honor
'eah`geitzich	covetous of honor
'eahlich	honest
'eahmlich	1. pitiful; 2. weak; 3. very sick
eahn/-d (f)	harvest; eahnda (pl)
'eahnda (g`eahnd)	to reap
eahnsht (m)	zeal
'eahnshtlich	1. earnest; 2. diligent
'eahnshtlichkeit (f)	1. earnestness; 2. diligence
'eahra (g`eaht) (ss)	to honor
eahsht	only now, only yet
eahsht	first
'eahshtah	formerly
'eahsht-frucht (f)	firstfruit; eahshti-frichta (pl)
'eahsht-ge`boahra	firstborn; eahsht-geboahrani (pl)
eaht (f)	earth; eahda (pl)
'eaht-`bayben (f)	earthquake; eaht-baybens (pl)
'eahtlich	earthly
'eahva (g`eahbt) (ss)	to inherit
'eahvah (m)	heir; eahvah (pl)
'eahvet (f)	1. work; 2. occupation; eahveda (pl)
eb	1. if, whether; 2. before
'ebbah	someone
'ebbes	something
'edlichi	quite a few
'eedah/endveddah	either, used with "adda" (or) to offer a choice between two alternatives
eem (dative case)	him
eems (m)	meal; eems (pl)

een	him
'eena (dative case)	them
'eesi	easy
eest	east
'eevil	evil
'eevil (neu)	evil; eevila (pl)
'eevil-`shaffah (m)	worker of evil; eevil-shaffah (pl)
`effan`gaylish	1. evangelistic; 2. Scriptural
`effan`gaylium (neu)	gospel
`effange`lisht (m)	evangelist; effangelishta (pl)
ei	1. (pref) in; 2. allied with;
	3. idiomatic
	interjection ex. "Ei, ich vays naett!"
	(Why, I don`t know!)
eich	you, accusative plural
'ei`denka (eigedenkt)	to keep in remembrance
'ei`drinka (eigedrunka)	to drink in
'ei`gay (eiganga)* (iv)	1. to associate with; 2. to shrink
'ei`gevva (eigevva) (ss)	to surrender, concede to
'ei`nemma (eignumma)	1. to take in; 2. to include
'ei`nemmah (m)	receiver; einemmah (pl)
'ei`rayna (eigraynd)	1. to rein in; 2. to restrain
'eisa (neu)	1. the substance of iron; 2. made of
	iron
'ei`samla (eiksammeld)	1. to gather in; 2. to harvest
'ei`seida (eikseit)	1. to agree with; 2. to side up with
'ei`seit/eisicht (f)	insight
'ei`setza (eiksetzt)	1. to ordain; 2. to establish in an of-
	fice; 3. to decree a ruling as law
'ei`shleesa (eikshlossa)	to lock in
'ei`shlohfa (eikshlohfa)*	to fall asleep
'ei`shpadda (eikshpatt)	to confine

'ei`shtekka (eikshtekt)	to incarcerate, imprison
'ei`shtimma (eikshtimd)	to agree or match with
'eisich	made of iron
'ei`sicht/eiseit (f)	insight; eisichta (pl)
'eiyah	your, plural
'eiyahlich	causing offense
'eiyahm (dative case)	your (plural)
'eiyahnis (neu)	something which causes offense; eiyahnisa (pl)
'eiyahra (geiyaht) (ss)	to speak offensively or argumentatively
'eiyetz	somewhere
ekk (neu)	corner; ekka/-h (pl)
'ekk-`shtay (m)	corner stone; ekk-shtay (pl)
eld (f)	age
'eldishtah (m)	elder in a church; eldishti (pl)
'eldlich	aged
'eldra (pl)	parents
elf	eleven
elft	eleventh
em	oneself (personal pronoun, accusative case)
em (dative case)	the
en	1. a, an; 2. unstressed form of "een" (him)
end	one of several
end (neu)	end; endah (pl)
'enda (g`end)	to end
'endlich	finally
'end`veddah/eedah	either; used with "adda" (or) to offer a choice between two alternatives
eng	narrow

21

'engel (m) — angel; engla (pl)

'engshtlich — anxious

'enkah (m) — anchor; enkah (pl)

'enkah-`hohka (m) — anchor hook; enkah-hohka (pl)

'ennich — any

es — 1. it; 2. the (neuter form); 3. she, her (when referring to unmarried girls) 4. that, who, which (relative pronoun)

esh (f) — ashes

'essa (gessa) — to eat

'essa (neu) — meal; essa (pl)

'essich (neu) — vinegar

'ess-`sach (neu) — food

'even — 1. indeed, actually; 2. nevertheless

'evvah — 1. ever, always; usually followed by "siddah" (since)

'evvahsht — uppermost

'extri — extra

F

fa — 1. for; 2. before

fa`achta (fa`acht) — 1. to despise, scorn; 2. to consider unimportant

fa`and`vadda (fa`andvatt) — 1. to answer; 2. to express

fa`and`vadlich — accountable

fa`aynicha (fa`aynicht) — to express agreement

fa`beeda (fabodda) — to forbid

fa`bei — past

fa`bessahra (fabessaht) (ss) — to improve

fa`biddahra (fabiddaht) (ss) — to grow bitter, disillusioned

fa`blenna (fablend) — to blind

fa`blohsa (fablohsa) — 1. to squander; 2. to blow away; 3. to burst

fa`bosta (fabost)	to burst
fa`brecha (fabrocha)	to break
fa`brenna (fabrend)	to burn
fa`dadda (fadatt)*	to wither
fa`damma (fadamd)	to condemn
fa`damnis (f)	condemnation; fadamnisa (pl)
fa`dauva(fadauva) /fadeahva (ss)	1. to damage; 2. to rot
fa`dayla (fadayld)	to separate
'faddel	quarter
'faddi	forward
'faddich	done
fa`deahva(fadeahva)/fadauva (ss)	1. to damage; 2. to rot
fa`deahving (f)	destruction
fa`deena (fadeend)	to earn
fa`deensht (m)	1. livelihood; 2. wages; 3. meritorious works
fa`dinga (fadunga)	to hire out oneself or another
fa`dinnahra (fadinnaht) (ss)	1. to thin out; 2. to dilute
fa`drauwa (fadraut) (ss)	to entrust
fa`drauwa (m)	confidence
fa`drayya (fadrayt)	1. to turn – usually negative in meaning, as to turn dials out of adjustment; 2. to twist the truth
fa`dredda (fadredda)	to trample underfoot
fa`drekka (fadrekt)	to soil or dirty
fa`drikka (fadrikt)	to squeeze or embrace, sometimes with excessive force
fa`drohsht (m)	confidence
fa`ennahra (fa`ennaht) (ss)	to change
fa`faula (fafauld)*	to spoil or rot
fa`fayla (fafayld)	to miss
fa`fiahra (fafiaht) (ss)	to deceive

23

fa`fiahrah (m)	one who deceives; fafiahrah (pl)
fa`fiahrah`rei (f)	1. deception; 2. the act of deception
fa`fiahrichkeit (f)	deceptiveness
fa`flucha (faflucht)	1. to place a curse on; 2. to swear at
fa`folka/-ya (fafolkt) (ss)	to persecute
fa`folya/-ka (fafolkt) (ss)	to persecute
fa`fressa	1. eaten away; 2. voracious
fa`gay (faganga)* (iv)	to disappear or evaporate
fa`gayshla (fagaysheld)	to lash or whip
fa`geesa (fagossa)	to pour out, spill
fa`gelshtahra (fagelshtaht)	to surprise or shock
fa`gessa (fagessa)	to forget
fa`gevva (fagevva) (ss)	to forgive
fa`gifta (fagift)	to poison
fa`glawwa (faglawkt) (ss)	1. to accuse or scold; 2. to complain about
fa`gleicha (faglicha)	to liken to
fa`gleichnis (f)	1. likeness; 2. parable; fagleichnissa (pl)
fa`globba (faglobt)	to beat up
fa`grawbnis (neu)	grave; fagrawbnissa (pl)
fa`grawva (fagrawva) (ss)	1. to bury; 2. to dig around in the ground
fa`grefticha (fagrefticht)	1. to strengthen; 2. to emphasize by using expletives
fa`gribbelda (pl)	crippled ones
fa`gribla (fagribbeld)	to cripple
fa`grumla (fagrummeld)	1. to scold; 2. to complain about
fa`gunna (fagunna)	1. to envy; 2. to desire misfortune for another
fa`gunnish/ fagunshtlich	1. envious; 2. malicious
fa`gunsht (m)	1. envy; 2. ill will

fa`gunshtlich/ fagunnish	1. envious; 2. malicious
fa`hadda (fahatt)	to harden
fa`halda (fahalda)	to prevent
fa`handla (fahandeld)	1. to discuss; 2. to trade
fa`hast	1. hateful; 2. to be hated
fa`heahra (faheaht) (ss)	to give a formal hearing or trial
fa`hexa (fahext)	1. to perform magic or sorcery; 2. to cast a spell or curse
fa`hinnahra (fahinnaht) (ss)	to hinder
fa`hudla (fahuddeld)	1. to confuse; 2. to disarray, clutter
fa`hungahra (fahungaht) (ss)	to starve
fa`immah	forever
fa`katza (fakatzt)	to shorten
fa`kawfa (fakawft)	to sell
fa`kindicha (fakindicht)	to proclaim, make known
fa`kleahra (fakleaht) (ss)	1. to glorify; 2. to clarify
fa`lacha (falacht)	1. to mock; 2. to esteem lightly, not take seriously
fa`langa (falangt)	to desire
fa`langa/ falanging (m)	desire; falanga (pl)
fa`langing/ falanga (f)	desire; falanginga (pl)
fa`laykla (falaykeld)	to deny
fa`layt	not eager, feeling reluctance
fald (f)	pleat; falda (pl)
fa`lengahra (falengaht) (ss)	to lengthen
fa`leshtahra (faleshtaht) (ss)	to blaspheme
fa`letza (faletzt)	to wrong
fa`liahra (faloahra) (ss)	to lose
falla (kfalla)*	to fall
fa`lossa (falossa)	1. to leave or go away from someone; 2. to depart; 3."falossa uf" (to rely on)
falsh	false

'falsh`hayt/-heit (f)	falsehood; falshhayda/-heida (pl)
'falsh`heit/-hayt (f)	falsehood; falshheida/-hayda (pl)
fa`lusht (m)	lust; falushta (pl)
fa`meahra (fameaht) (ss)	to increase
fa`meika (fameikt)	1. to notice; 2. to make marks on
fa`mohna (famohnd)	to admonish
fa`mohning (f)	admonition; famohninga (pl)
fa`nemma (fanumma)	to perceive
'fanga (kfanga)	to catch
'fang-`shtrikk (m)	snare; fang-shtrikk (pl)
'fanna	in front, at the front
'fanna-`heah	ahead of
'fannich	1. in front of; 2. funny
fa`rayya (faraykt) (ss)	to move
fa`reisa (farissa)	to tear
fa`robba (farobt)	to pull apart into many pieces
fa`rohda (farohda)	to betray
fa`roshta (farosht)*	to rust
fa`samla (fasammeld)	to gather, to assemble
fa`saufa (fasoffa)	to drown
fa`savvahra (fasavvaht) (ss)	to sour
fa`seiya (faseikt) (ss)	to take care of
fa`senka (fasenkt)	to singe, burn
fa`shelda (fasholda)	to scold, berate
fa`shlauwa (fashlauwa) (ss)	to beat up
fa`shleesa (fashlossa)	to completely lock up
fa`shmelsa (fashmolsa)	to melt
fa`shmiahra (fashmiaht) (ss)	to smear
fa`shohma (fashohmd)	to shame, mock
fa`shpalda (fashpalda)	to split apart
fa`shpodda (fashpott)	to mock
fa`shprecha (fashprocha)	to promise

fa`shpreching/fashprechnis (f)	promise; fashprechnissa (pl)
fa`shprechnis/fashpreching (f)	promise; fashprechinga (pl)
fa`shrekka (fashrokka)	to scare
fasht	almost
'fashta (kfasht)	to fast
fa`shtand (m)	1. moderation, decency; 2. understanding
fa`shtatza (fashtatzt)	1. to confuse; 2. to cause to stumble
fa`shtauna (fashtaund)	to astonish
fa`shtay (fashtanna) (iv)	to understand
'fasht-`dawk (m)	day of fasting; fasht-dawwa (pl)
fa`shteika (fashteikt)	to strengthen
fa`shteiking (f)	oath; fashteikinga (pl)
fa`shtekla (fashtekkeld)	to hide
fa`shtella (fashteld)	to alter one's appearance in order to deceive
fa`shtelling (f)	false appearance; fashtellinga (pl)
fa`shtendich/-lich	reasonable
fa`shtendlichkeit (f)	reasonableness
fa`shtendnis (f)	comprehension, understanding
fa`shtikka (fashtikt)	1. to suffocate; 2. to smother
fa`shtokt	stubborn
fa`shtroiya (fashtroit)	to scatter
fa`shuah	for sure, assuredly
fa`shuldicha (fashuldicht)	1. to accuse; 2. to transgress against
fa`shveahra (fashveaht) (ss)	to forswear
fa`shvetza (fashvetzt)	1. to discuss; 2. to persuade by talking
'fassich	forward
fa`sucha (fasucht)	1. to tempt; 2. to attempt; 3. to taste
fa`suchah (m)	tempter
fatt	away
'fat`zay	fourteen

27

'fat`zayt	fourteenth
'fatzich	forty
faul	1. lazy; 2. rotten
'faul`ensah (m)	lazy person: faulensah (pl)
fausht (f)	fist; feisht (pl)
fa`vanna (favand)	to warn
fa`vass	why
fa`velka (favelkt)*	to wither, wilt
fa`vunnahra (favunnaht) (ss)	to astonish
'fawbel (f)	fable; fawbla (pl)
fa`yawwa (fayawkt) (ss)	to disturb or chase
fayl	1. defect, fault; 2. "unni fayl," doubtless; faylah (pl)
'fayla (kfayld)	to fail
'faylah (m)	1. error; 2. sickness; faylah (pl)
'faylah-`suchah (m)	(lit. fault seeker) fault finder; faylah-suchah (pl)
fa`zayla (fazayld)	to tell or narrate
fa`zeahra (fazeaht) (ss)	to consume, as by fire
fa`zeahrich	consuming
fecht (f)	fight; fechta (pl)
'fechta (kfochta)	to fight
'fechtah (m)	fighter; fechtah (pl)
'feddah (m)	feather; feddahra (pl)
'feddahsht	forward most
fee (neu)	livestock
'feedahra (kfeedaht) (ss)	to feed
feel	1. many; 2. much
'feela (kfeeld)	to feel
fei	1. very small or fine; 2. fancy
'feicha (kfeicht)	to fear
'feich`butzich	fearful

28

'feicht`lohs	fearless
feind (m)	enemy; feinda (pl)
'feiya (pl)	figs
'feiya-`bohm (m)	fig tree; feiya-baym (pl)
'feiyah (neu)	fire; feiyahra (pl)
'feiyah-`dawk (m)	holiday; feiyah-dawwa (pl)
'feiyah-`flamm (neu)	flame of fire; feiyah-flamma (pl)
'feiyah-`offa (m)	fire oven; feiyah-effa (pl)
'feiyahrich	fiery
'feiyah-`shtekka (m)	(lit. fire stick) torch; feiyah-shtekka (pl)
feld (neu)	field; feldah (pl)
'felsa (m)	boulder, rock; felsa (pl)
'felsa-`loch (neu)	(lit. rock hole) cave; felsa-lechah (pl)
fens (f)	fence; fensa (pl)
'fenshtah (neu)	window; fenshtahra (pl)
fesht	fastened, connected to
fesht (neu)	religious holiday feast; feshta (pl)
fett	fat
fett (neu)	lard
fiah	four
'fiah-`ekkich	having four corners
'fiah-`feesich	four-footed
'fiahra (kfiaht) (ss)	to lead
'fikkahra (kfikkaht) (ss)	1. to calculate; 2. to plan on
'filla (kfild)	to fill
fimf	five
'fingah (m)	finger; fingah (pl)
'finna (kfunna)	to find
'finshtahnis (f)	darkness
'fisha (kfisht)	to fish
'fishah (m)	one who fishes; fishah (pl)

29

'fish-`lein (f)	fish line; fish-leina (pl)
fitz (f)	1. twig; 2. whip; fitza (pl)
flamm (neu)	flame; flamma (pl)
flaysh (neu)	flesh
'flayshlich	fleshly
'flaysh-`market (m)	meat market; flaysh-markets (pl)
'fleeya (kflohwa)* (ss)	1. to fly; 2. to flee
fleicht	maybe
'fleisich	diligent
'fleisichkeit (f)	diligence
'flekka (m)	1. spot, stain; 2. particle of matter
'flexa (pl)	sinews, tendons
'flikka (kflikt)	to mend
'flikkel (m)	wing; flikla (pl)
floah (m)	floor; floahra (pl)
flott (f)	flood; flots (pl)
fluch (m)	curse; flucha (pl)
'flucha (kflucht)	to swear, curse
foah	forth
'foah`bild (neu)	example; foahbildah (pl)
'foah`bilda (foahgebild)	to set an example or pattern
'foah`denkes (neu)	(lit. thinking ahead) foresight
'foah`eldra (pl)	forefathers
'foah`faddah (m)	forefather; foahfeddah (pl)
'foah`gang (m)	1. preeminence; 2. example
'foah`gay (foahganga)* (iv)	to lead
'foah`gayyah (m)	leader; foahgayyah (pl)
'foah`gengah (m)	leader; foahgengah (pl)
'foah`gukka (foahgegukt)	to look ahead
'foah`heah	earlier, before a specified time
'foah`naymsht	preeminent, most important
'foahra (kfoahra) (ss)	1. to drive; 2. to ride; 3. to haul

'foah`richta (foahgricht)	to predetermine
'foah`rishta (foahgrisht)	to prepare ahead
'foah`roofa (foahgroofa)	to choose ahead of time
foahs (m)	force
'foah`sawwa (foahksawt) (ss)	to predict, prophesy
'foah`setza (foahksetzt)	1. to set in a position of eminence; 2. to set forth
'foah`shtella (foahkshteld)	to set forth
'foah`sicht (f)	foresight
'foah`vissa (foahgvist) (iv)	to know ahead of time
'foah`vitzich	bossy, presumptuous
'foah`zayla (foahgezayld)	to plan ahead
'foah`zeit (f)	earlier time; foahzeida (pl)
'fokkel (m)	bird; fekkel/feyyel (pl)
fol`filla (folkfild)	to fulfill
'fol`heit (f)	fulness
folk (neu)	people, nation
'fol`kumma	perfect
'fol`kummaheit (f)	fulness, perfection
foll	full
'fol`shtendich/-lich	fully
'folya (kfolkt)* (ss)	to follow
'foodah-`drohk (m)	manger; foodah-drayk (pl)
foos (m)	foot; fees (pl)
'foos-`dabba (pl)	footsteps
'foos-`shtool (m)	footstool; foos-shteel (pl)
fox (m)	fox; fix (pl)
'fransel (m)	1. fringe; 2. ragged thread; fransla (pl)
fraw (f)	1. wife; 2. woman; frawwa (pl)
'fraylich	joyful
'fraylichkeit (f)	joyfulness
frayt (f)	joy

free	early
frei	free
'frei-`drayyah (m)	deliverer; frei-drayyah (pl)
'frei`heit (f)	freedom
freind (m)	1. friend; 2. relative; friend (pl)
'freindlich	friendly
'freindlichkeit (f)	friendliness
'freind`shaft (f)	relatives
'freind`shaft-re`gishtah (m)	genealogy; freindshaft-registahra (pl)
'freind`shaft-`shtamm (m)	genealogy; freindshaft-shtemm (pl)
'frei-`shtelling (f)	deliverance
'frei-`villich	voluntarily
fremd	1. unfamiliar; 2. strange, unusual
'fressa (kfressa)	1. to eat (animals only); 2. to overeat; 3. to eat too fast or impolitely
'fressah (m)	glutton
'fressah`rei (f)	gluttony
'freyyaheit (f)	joy
'fridda (m)	peace
'fridlich	peacefully, peaceful
frish	fresh
froh	glad
frohk (m)	question; frohwa (pl)
'frohwa (kfrohkt) (ss)	to ask
'froiya (kfroit) (ss)	to rejoice
fromm	pious
frosh (m)	frog; fresh (pl)
fuah (f)	1. team of horses or oxen; 2. a horse and carriage in hitch; fuahra (pl)
frucht (f)	fruit; frichta (pl)
'fruchtboah	fruitful
'frucht-`feld (neu)	field with a crop in it; frucht-feldah (pl)

32

'fuddah (m)	in buildings – the foundation wall which extends below the frost line; fuddahs (pl)
'fuft`zay	fifteen
'fuftzich	fifty
fu`m	of the
'fuma	of a
funn	1. of; 2. from
'funn-`nannah	separate from each other
'funn`ra	of a
furcht (f)	fear

G

gall (f)	1. gallon; 2. gall; galla (pl)
gans	entire, whole
gans (f)	goose; gens (pl)
gaul (m)	horse; geil (pl)
gay (ganga)* (iv)	to go
'gaygend (f)	1. community 2. area; gaygenda (pl)
gayl	yellow
gays (m)	goat; gays (pl)
'gaysa-`haut (f)	goatskin; gaysa-heit (pl)
'gayshel (f)	whip, scourge; gayshla (pl)
'gayshla (gegaysheld)	to scourge or whip
'gayshtling (f)	scourging; gayshtlinga (pl)
geahn	1. gladly; 2. with desire
geahsht (f)	barley
'geahsht-`broht (neu)	barley bread
ge`bayt (neu)	prayer; gebaydah (pl)
ge`bei (neu)	building; gebeiyah (pl)
ge`biss (neu)	mouthpiece of a bridle, bit; gebissah (pl)

ge`boahra *	born
ge`bott (neu)	command; gebodda (pl)
ge`braekk (neu)	the act of bragging
ge`brauch (m)	1. custom; 2. habit; gebraucha (pl)
ge`breddich (neu)	preaching, teaching
ge`danka (pl)	thoughts
ge`dawf (neu)	the practice of baptizing
'geddahra (gegeddaht) (ss)	to gather
ge`duld/geduldheit (f)	patience
ge`duldheit/geduld (f)	patience
ge`duldich	patient, forbearing
'geedichkeit (f)	kindness, benevolence
ge`fecht (neu)	habitual fighting
'geils-`mann (m)	horseman; geils-mennah (pl)
Geisht (m)	the Holy Spirit
geisht (m)	spirit; geishtah (pl)
'geishtlich	spiritual
'geishtlichkeit (f)	spirituality
geitz (m)	covetousness
'geitzich	covetous
geld (neu)	money
'geld-`box (f)	donation box; geld-boxa (pl)
'geld-`sakk (m)	money bag; geld-sekk (pl)
'geld-`vexlah (m)	money changer; geld-vexlah (pl)
ge`leebt	beloved
ge`leshtah	habitual blaspheming
ge`nunk	enough
ge`recht	righteous
ge`rechtichkeit (f)	righteousness
ge`richt (neu)	judgment; gerichta (pl)
ge`richtichkeit (f)	judgment
ge`richts-dawk (m)	judgment day; gerichts-dawwa (pl)

34

'geshtah	yesterday
ge'shtayl (neu)	habitual stealing
'gettin (f)	goddess
'getlich	godly
'getlichkeit (f)	godliness
'getza-'opfah (neu)	offering made to an idol; getza-opfahra (pl)
ge'vislich	surely, undoubtedly
ge'viss	for sure
'gevva (gevva) (ss)	1. to give; 2. to happen
'gevvah (m)	giver; gevvah (pl)
'gevvich	I give
'geyya	1. steep; 2. against, opposed to; 3. toward
'geyyich	1. against, opposed to; 2. toward
ge'zahh (neu)	arguing, debating
'gichtahra (pl)	seizures, convulsions
gift (neu)	poison
'giftich	poisonous
glantz (m)	brightness
glatt	smooth
glawk (f)	1. complaint; 2. accusation; glawwa (pl)
glaws (neu)	1. glass, the material; 2. water glass; glessah (pl)
'glawsich	1. made of glass; 2. glassy
'glawva (geglawbt) (ss)	1. to believe; 2. to be of the opinion
'glawva (m)	1. faith; 2. belief; 3. religion; glawva (pl)
'glawvich	1. believing, having faith; 2. I believe
'glawwa (geglawkt) (ss)	to complain
glay	small, tiny; glennah, glensht
'glayda (geglayt)	to clothe

35

'glaydah	clothing
'glaydah-`sakk (m)	garment bag; glaydah-sekk (pl)
glayt (neu)	garment; glaydah (pl)
gleet (neu)	member; gleedah (pl)
glei	soon
'gleich/-a/-lich	1. same, identical; 2. equal
'gleicha (geglicha)	to like
'gleicha` veis	likewise
'gleichnis (neu)	1. parable; 2. likeness; gleichnissa (pl)
'gleyyaheit (f)	1. opportunity; 2. privilege; gleyyaheida (pl)
'glitzahrich	glittering
'gloahheit (f)	1. glory; 2. clearness
'globba (geglobt)	1. to beat; 2. to knock on a door
glukk (f)	setting hen; glukka (pl)
'glumba (m)	lump, clump; glumba (pl)
'glushta (geglusht)	to desire
'glushta (m)	desire; glushta (pl)
'glushtich	desirous (adj.)
gmay (f)	1. church, group of believers; 2. worship service; gmayna (pl)
'gmay-`haus (neu)	church house; gmay-heisah (pl)
'gmein`shaft (f)	fellowship
'gmohna (gegmohnd)	1. to seem; 2. to remind
'gnawda-`shtool (m)	mercy seat (theological)
'gnawdi/ gnawt (f)	grace
gnawt/ gnawdi (f)	grace
gnecht (m)	servant; gnechta (pl)
'gnechta-`geisht (m)	spirit or attitude of servanthood
'gnecht`shaft (f)	servanthood
gnee (neu)	knee; gnee (pl)

'gnocha (m)	bone; gnocha (pl)
goah	completely, entirely
'goahra (m)	garden; goahra (pl)
'goahra-`haldah (m)	gardener; goahra-haldah (pl)
'goldich	golden
goot	good; bessah, besht
'goot-`maynich	kind, well meaning
'goot-`maynichkeit (f)	kindness; goot-maynichkeida (pl)
'goot-`shmakkich	having a good smell
Gott (m)	God; gettah (pl)
'Gottes-`deensht (m)	1. worship service; 2. the act of serving God
'Gottes-`furcht (f)	fear of God
'Gott-`firchtich	God fearing
'Gottheit (f)	Godhead
'gott`lohs	ungodly
grabb (f)	crow; grabba (pl)
'gradla (gegraddeld)*	to crawl
'graebba (gegraebt)	to grab
graft (f)	strength; grefta (pl)
grank	sick
'granket/-heit (f)	sickness; grankada/-heida (pl)
'grausam/-lich	revolting, repulsive
'grauslich/-sam	revolting, repulsive
grawb (neu)	grave; grayvah (pl)
grawt	1. straight; 2. immediately; 3. directly; 4. exactly
'grawt`zu	by shortcut
'grawva (gegrawva) (ss)	to dig
'grawva (m)	1. ditch; 2. gully; 3. crevice; grawva (pl)
'grayya (gegrayt)	to crow (as a rooster)

37

gree	green
'greedich	greedy
greek (m)	war; greeka (pl)
'greeks-`deenah (m)	military employee; greeks-deenah (pl)
'greeks-`gaul (m)	war horse; greeks-geil (pl)
'greeks-`gnecht (m)	soldier; greeks-gnechta (pl)
'greeks-`hauptman (m)	military captain; greeks-hauptmennah (pl)
'greeks-`hoot (m)	helmet; greeks-heet (pl)
'greeks-`ksha (neu)	armor; greeks-ksharra (pl)
'greeks-`leit (pl)	army people
'greeks-`mann (m)	soldier; greeks-mennah (pl)
'greesa (gegreest)	to greet
'greeya (grikt) (iv)	to get
'greeyish	Greek (adjective)
'grefta (f)	strength
'greftich	1. strong; 2. hearty
'greftichlich	1. strongly; 2. heartily
'greidah (f)	herbs
'greidah-`ayl (neu)	ointment
'greilich	abominable
'greisha (gegrisha)	to yell or scream
'greislich	vile
greitz (neu)	cross; greitza (pl)
'greitzicha (gegreitzicht)	to crucify
'gribbel (m)	cripple; gribla (pl)
'gribla (gegribbeld)	to cripple
grikk (f)	1. brook; 2. crutch; grikka (pl)
'grimmel (f)	crumb; grimla (pl)
grish (m)	shout; grisha (pl)
'Grishta-`mensh (m)	Christian person; Grishta-leit (pl)
'Grishtlich	pertaining to the Christian faith

38

grohs	big; graysah, graysht
'grohs-`feelich	conceited, arrogant
'grohs-`mammi (f)	grandmother; grohs-mammis (pl)
'groofa	called out, chosen
groos (m)	greeting
'grosha (m)	small coin, penny; grosha (pl)
'grumla (gegrummeld)	to grumble
'grumlah (m)	grumbler; grumlah (pl)
grumm	crooked, not straight
grund (m)	1. ground; 2. the reason or basis for an action or belief
'grunda (gegrund)	1. to establish, ground; 2. to found
'grund-loch (neu)	hole in the earth, den; grund-lechah (pl)
'gukka (gegukt)	to look
gvald (f)	power, strength
'gvaldich	powerful
'gvayla (gegvayld)	to torment
'gvayl-blatz (m)	place of torment; gvayl-bletz (pl)
'gvayna (gegvaynd)	to get used to
'gvaynlich	customarily
'gveahva (gegveahvt)	to squirm
'gveahva (pl)	joints of bones
gvest	was, were, used with "sei" to create past perfect tense
gvicht (f)	weight; gvichta (pl)
'gviddah (m)	lightning
'gviddah-`shtoahm (m)	thunderstorm; gviddah-shtoahms (pl)
'gvissa (neu)	conscience; gvissa (pl)
'gvunna	1. won; 2. persuaded
'gvunnahrich	curious

H

'haendla (kaendeld)	to handle
'haffa (m)	pot, crock; haffa (pl)
Hah (m)	Lord; hahra (pl)
hakk (f)	1. hoe; 2. a striking blow; 3. an insulting remark; hakka (pl)
hakka (kakt)	to hoe
halb	half
'halb-`nacht (f)	midnight
'halda (kalda)	to keep
'hallich	glorious
'hallichkeit (f)	glory; hallichkeida (pl)
hals (m)	1. neck; 2. throat; hels (pl)
'hamli (neu)	calf; hamlen (pl)
hand (f)	hand; hend (pl)
'handla (kandeld)	1. to deal with; 2. to trade
'hand-`lumba (m)	towel; hand-lumba (pl)
'hand-`shreives (neu)	handwriting
hann (f)	horn; hanna (pl)
harf (f)	harp; harfa (pl)
'harf-`shpeelah (m)	harp player; harf-shpeelah (pl)
'hassa (kast)	to hate
hatt	hard
'hatt-`heahrich	hard of hearing
'hatt-`shaffich	hardworking
hatz (neu)	heart; hatza (pl)
'hatzlich	heartfelt
'haufa	many, always preceded by "en" (a, an)
'haufa (m)	pile; heifa (pl)
'hauptmann (m)	captain; hauptmennah (pl)
haus	1. out here; 2. escaped
haus (neu)	house; heisah (pl)

40

'haus-`dach (neu) — house roof; haus-dechah (pl)

'haus-`faddah (m) — the father or master of the house; hausfeddah (pl)

'haus-`haldah (m) — steward; haus-haldah (pl)

'haus-`haldes (neu) — stewardship

'haus-`halding (f) — 1. household; 2. stewardship; haus-haldinga (pl)

'haus-`hohf (m) — courtyard; haus-hohfa (pl)

'haus-`hohld (neu) — household; haus-hohlda (pl)

'havva (kat) (iv) — to have

'havvich — I have

hay (f) — a raised location (hay is always prefixed by "in di" [in the])

haych (f) — height; haycha (pl)

'hayla (kayld) — to heal

haym — toward home

'haymet (f) — home; haymedah (pl)

hays — hot

'haysa (kaysa) — 1. to invite; 2. to call, name; 3. to be called, named

'hayva (kohva) (ss) — to hold

heah — toward here

'heahra (keaht) (ss) — 1. to hear; 2. to belong

'heahrich — 1. I hear; 2. I belong; 3. hearing ability; ex. "hatt-heahrich" (hard of hearing)

'hedda — would have

hee — toward there

'heeda (keet) — 1. to beware of; 2. to take care of

'heedah (m) — one who takes care of; heedah (pl)

'heicha (keicht) — 1. to obey; 2. to listen

'heichlah (m) — hypocrite; heichlah (pl)

Heid (m)	Gentile; Heida (pl)
'heidich's	used only in the phrase "heidich's dawk" (nowadays)
'heifla (keifeld)	to pile together
'heila (keild)	to weep
'Heiland (m)	the Saviour, Jesus Christ
'heilich	holy
'heilicha (keilicht)	to sanctify
'heilsam	wholesome
heit	today
'heiyahra (keiyaht) (ss)	to marry
hekk (f)	a branch or twig; hekka (pl)
'hekka-`putsha (m)	clump of bushes; hekka-putsha (pl)
'helfa (kolfa)	to help
'helfah (m)	helper; helfah (pl)
helft	half; helfta (pl)
hell	1. light colored; 2. used to describe a piercing quality in noise; 3. of light – very bright
hell (f)	hell
'hell-`feiyah (neu)	hell fire; hell-feiyahra (pl)
'helling (f)	light, and/or its properties
'hellish	pertaining to hell
hemm (neu)	shirt; hemmah (pl)
'henka (kanka)	to hang
'heslich	extremely, very
hett	would have
'hetza (ketzt)	to incite
'hexah (m)	sorcerer; hexah (pl)
'hexa`hrei (neu)	sorcery
hift (f)	hip; hifda (pl)

hilf (f)	assistance
'himlish	heavenly
'Himmel (m)	heaven; himla (pl)
'Himmel-`reich (neu)	kingdom of heaven
'Himmels-`broht (neu)	showbread
'Himmels-`grefta (pl)	powers of heaven
'Himmelshaft (f)	heavenly establishment; Himmel-shafda (pl)
'hinna	located to the back
'hinnahnis (neu)	hindrance; hinnahnissa (pl)
'hinnahsht	farthest to the back
'hinnahsich	backward
'hinnich	behind
hitz (f)	heat
'hivvel (m)	hill; hivvela (pl)
hoah (f)	hair; hoah (pl)
'hocht`zeidah/ hochtzich-mann (m)	bridegroom; hochtzeidah (pl)
'hochtzich (f)	wedding; hochtzicha (pl)
'hochtzich-`leit	people in a wedding party
'hochtzich-`mann/ hochtzeidah (m)	bridegroom; hochtzich-mennah (pl)
'hochtzich-`maydel (neu)	bride; hochtzich-mayt (pl)
'hoffa (koft)	to hope
'hofning (f)	hope; hofninga (pl)
hohch	1. high; 2. not Amish; haychah, haychsht
'hohch-`engel (m)	archangel; hoch-engela (pl)
'hohch-`gacht	highly esteemed
'hohch-ge`boahra	of noble birth
'hohch-ge`lohbt	highly praised
'hohch`meedich	proud, haughty
'hohch`moot (m)	pride
hohf (m)	yard; hohfa (pl)

43

'hohla (kohld)	to fetch
'hohna (m)	rooster; hohna (pl)
hoi (neu)	hay
'hoi-`shrekk (m)	grasshopper; hoi-shrekka (pl)
'hokka (kokt)	to sit
hols (neu)	wood
'holsich	wooden
'huah (f)	prostitute; huahra (pl)
'huahra (kuaht) (ss)	to indulge in debauchery
'huahrah (m)	one who indulges in debauchery; huahrah (pl)
'huahra`rei (neu)	prostitution
hund (m)	dog; hund (pl)
'hungah (m)	hunger
'hungahrich	hungry
'hungahs-`noht (f)	famine; hungahs-nohda (pl)
'hunna	down here
'hunnaht	hundred
'hunnich (neu)	honey
hutsh (m)	colt; hutsha (pl)

I

'iahra	1. her, hers; 2. their, theirs; 3. to her
ich	I
im	in the
'imma	contraction of "im en" (in a)
'immah	always
in	in
'in`dressa (f)	interest (financial)
in`geyya	1. headed in the direction of; 2. contrary to one`s will or desire
'innahlich	inward

'innen	in a
'in`seid	inside
'insens-`awldah (m)	incense altar; insens-awldahra (pl)
'insens-`kobli (neu)	incense cup; insens-koblen (pl)
'in`vendich	on the inside
is	is
'ivvah	1. past; 2. over, above; 3. again
'ivvah-`beeya (ivvah-gebohwa) (ss)	to bend over
'ivvah-`deenah (m)	commanding officer; ivvah-deenah (pl)
'ivvah-`dekka (ivvah-gedekt)	to cover over
'ivvah demm	then, at that time
'ivvah-`denka (ivvah-gedenkt)	to think over
'ivvah-di`maws	extremely, beyond measure
'ivvah-`drayya (ivvah-gedrayt)	to turn over
'ivvah-`dredda (ivvah-gedredda)	to trespass
'ivvah-`dreddah (m)	one who trespasses; ivah-dreddah (pl)
'ivvah-`dredding (f)	trespass; ivvah-dreddinga (pl)
'ivvah-`gevva (ivvah-gevva) (ss)	to give control of a matter to another
'ivvah-`gukka (ivvah-gegukt)	1. to look over; 2. to overlook; 3. to disregard purposely
'ivvah-`hand (f)	dominance
'ivvah-`hemm (neu)	coat; ivvah-hemmah (pl)
'ivvah-`kumma (ivvah-kumma)*	to overcome
'ivvah-`kummah (m)	overcomer; ivvah-kummah (pl)
'ivvah-`lawfa (ivvah-gloffa)*	to run over, overflow
'ivvah-`layya (ivvah-glaykt) (ss)	to overlay, cover
'ivvah-`lossa (ivvah-glost)	to leave control of a matter to another
'ivvah-`macha (ivvah-gmacht)	to make again
'ivvah-`macht (f)	supreme power; ivvah-machta (pl)
'ivvah-`mechtich	supremely powerful
'ivvah-`meiya	day after tomorrow
'ivvah-`nacht	overnight

45

'ivvah-`nemma (ivvah-gnumma)	1. to take over; 2. to overtake
'ivvah`raus	to a great extent
'ivvahrawl	everywhere
'ivvahrich	left over
'ivvah-`rokk (m)	a heavy outer coat; ivvah-rekk (pl)
'ivvah-`sayna (ivvah-ksenna)	to oversee
'ivvah-`saynah (m)	overseer; ivvah-saynah (pl)
'ivvah-`setza (ivvah-ksetzt)	1. to translate; 2. to put in charge
'ivvah-`vinna (ivvah-gvunna)	1. to win over, persuade; 2. to conquer

K

kalb (neu)	calf; kelvah (pl)
kald	cold; keldah, keldsht
kall (m)	fellow; kals (pl)
ka`mayl (m)	camel; kamayla (pl)
'kammah (f)	a room; kammahra (pl)
kann (f)	1. kernel, grain; 2. vessel for carrying liquid
kann (iv)	can, to be able to
'kashta (m)	1. chest; 2. bin; kashta (pl)
katt	had
katz	short
katz (f)	cat; katza (pl)
'katzlich	recently
'kawfa (gekawft)	to buy
'kawf-`haus (neu)	market building; kawf-heisah (pl)
'kawf-`leit (pl)	merchants
'kayfah (m)	merchant; kayfah (pl)
'kaynich (m)	king; kaynicha (pl)
'kaynich-`eah (f)	majesty
'kaynich-`shtool (m)	throne; kaynich-shteel (pl)

'kaynichs-`sohn (m)	prince; kaynichs-sayna (pl)
'keahra (gekeaht) (ss)	to sweep
'kebba (gekebt)	to behead
keel	cool
'keela (gekeeld)	to cool
'keishheit (f)	chastity
'kemma (gekemd)	to comb
'kemmahrah (m)	eunuch; kemmahrah (pl)
kend	would be able to
kenn	none, not any
'kenna (gekend)	to recognize or know someone or something
kens	none, not any
'keshtlich	precious
'kessel (m)	kettle, pot; kesla (pl)
kett (f)	chain; kedda (pl)
'kfeahlich	dangerous
kfeel (neu)	1. good will or bad will in a group; 2. feeling or sensation; kfeelah (pl)
'kfellich	approved of
'kfengnis (neu)	jail; kfengnissa (pl)
kfoah (f)	danger; kfoahra (pl)
kind (neu)	child; kinnah (pl)
'kindish	childish, silly
'kinnah-`eahbshaft (f)	inheritance of children; kinnah-eahb-shafta (pl)
'kins-`kind (f)	grandchild; kins-kinnah (pl)
'kissa (gekist)	to kiss
'kissi (neu)	pillow; kissis (pl)
kliah	clear
'klinglich	tinkling
koahb (m)	basket; keahb (pl)

47

'koahb-`foll (m)   basket full; keahb-foll (pl)

kobb (m)   head; kebb (pl)

'kobb-`feddahsht   headfirst

'kobli (neu)   cup; koblen (pl)

'kocha (gekocht)   to cook

kohl (f)   coal; kohla (pl)

'kolva (m)   ear or cob of corn; kolva (pl)

'koshta (gekosht)   to cost

'koshtboah   costly

kotz (m)   vomit

'kotza (gekotzt)   to vomit

krohn (m)   crown; krohna (pl)

'krohna (gekrohnd)   to crown

ksetz (neu)   1. law; 2. the Old Testament law; ksetza (pl)

'ksetz-`brechah (m)   breaker of the law; ksetz-brechah (pl)

'ksetz-`gevvah (m)   law giver; ksetz-gevvah (pl)

ksetzt   1. appointed, set; 2. heavy-set

ksha (neu)   1. dishes; 2. harness; ksharra (pl)

ksheft (neu)   work, deed; kshefta (pl)

ksheit   reasonable, moderate

kshenk (neu)   gift; kshenka/-ah (pl)

'kshenkah-`geld (neu)   donation, offering

kshicht (f)   1. happening; 2. story; kshichta (pl)

kshlecht (neu)   1. generation; 2. ethnic group; kshlechtah (pl)

kshmakk (m)   scent, smell; kshmakka (pl)

'kshpassich   strange, unusual

kshpukk (m)   ghost; kshpukka (pl)

kshveah (f)   a boil or sore; kshveahra (pl)

kshvetz (neu)   1. manner of talking; 2. rumor; kshvetzah (pl)

'kshvilla (kshvulla)*	to swell
kshvind	quick
'kshvissich	between
ksicht (neu)	face; ksichtah (pl)
'ksoffa	intoxicated
ksund	healthy
'ksundhayt (f)	health
'kubbah (neu)	copper
'kubbah-`shmitt (m)	coppersmith; kubbah-shmidda (pl)
'kumma (kumma)*	to come
'kum`rawt (m)	1. comrade; kumrawda (pl); 2. gear wheel; kumreddah (pl)
kuss (m)	kiss; kuss (pl)

L

'lacha (glacht)	to laugh
la`dann (f)	lantern; ladanna (pl)
lamm (neu)	lamb; lemmah (pl)
land (neu)	land; lendah (pl)
'land`shaft (neu)	1. region; 2. landscape, topography; landshafta (pl)
'lands-`leit (pl)	native inhabitants
lang	long; lengah, lengsht
'langa (glangt)	to reach
'lanna (gland)	1. to learn; 2. to teach
'lanning (f)	1. teaching or doctrine; 2. education; lanninga (pl)
lasht (f)	1. burden; 2. reluctance to perform a task; lashta (pl)
latt	lot, many
latt (f)	wood strip, lath; ladda (pl)
'lauda (glaut)	to sound or appear to someone

49

laut	loud
lawb (neu)	foliage
'lawb-`haus (neu)	ceremonial hut built of branches; lawb heisah (pl)
'lawda (glawda)	to load
'lawda (m)	shelf; lawda (pl)
'lawfa (gloffa)*	to walk
lawt (f)	coffin; lawda (pl)
layb (m)	1. loaf; layb (pl); 2. lion; layva (pl)
'laydich	bored, tired of, fed up
'layna (glaynd)	1. to borrow; 2. to lend
'laynich	alone
'layns-`leit (f)	money lenders
'laysa (glaysa)	to read
'laysah (m)	one who reads; laysah (pl)
'layva (glaybt) (ss)	to live
'layva (neu)	life; layva (pl)
'layves-`buch (neu)	Book of Life
'layves-`krohn (m)	crown of life
'layves-`lang	entire life span
'layves-`lawf (m)	walk of life, conduct
'layves-`mawl (neu)	nourishment
'layves-`zeit (f)	lifetime
'layya (glaykt) (ss)	to lay
leah	empty; leahrah, leahsht
'leahra (gleaht) (ss)	1. to pour; 2. to teach
'leahrah (m)	1. teacher; 2. preacher; leahrah (pl)
'lebbish	lukewarm
'leddah (neu)	1. leather; 2. made of leather
'leddich	not married, unattached
leeb	dear, beloved
'leebens`mawl (neu)	religious love feast

'leeblich	beloved
leek (m)	lie, untruth; leeya (pl)
leet (neu)	song; leedah (pl)
'leeva (gleebt) (ss)	to love
'leevah	rather, preferably
'leevah (m)	lever; leevahra (pl)
'leevich	beloved
'leeya (gleekt) (ss)	to lie, tell an untruth
'leeyah/ liknah (m)	one who lies; leeyah (pl)
left (f)	lip; leftza (pl)
leib (m)	body; leivah (pl)
'leiblich	pertaining to the body
leicht	1. light, not heavy; 2. light colored
leicht (f)	funeral; leichta (pl)
'leicht-`hatzich	lighthearted, unconcerned, insincere
'leicht-`leet (neu)	funeral song; leicht-leedah (pl)
'leida (glidda)	to suffer
leit (f)	people
'leiya (gleyya) (ss)	to lie, assume a prone position
leng (f)	length; leng (pl)
'leshtah-`diah (neu)	beast that blasphemes; leshtah-diahra (pl)
'leshtah-`nohma (m)	name of blasphemy; leshtah-nayma (pl)
'leshtahra (gleshtaht)	to blaspheme
'leshtahrah (m)	one who blasphemes; leshtahrah (pl)
'leshtah-`vatt (neu)	word of blasphemy; leshtah-vadda (pl)
letsht	last
letz	wrong
le`vendich	alive (form)
'levvich	alive

51

licht (neu)	light; lichtah (pl)
'licht-`shtaend (m)	lightstand; licht-shtaenda (pl)
'liknah/ leeyah (m)	liar; liknah (pl)
'lilya-`blumm (f)	lily; lilya-blumma (pl)
lings	1. on or toward the left; 2. left-handed
'linnen-`duch (neu)	linen fabric
loch (neu)	hole; lechah (pl)
lohb (neu)	praise
'lohb-`breef (m)	letter of praise; lohb-breefa (pl)
'lohb-`leet (neu)	song of praise; lohb-leedah (pl)
'lohb-`opfah (neu)	sacrifice of praise; lohb-opfahra (pl)
lohm	lame
lohn (m)	wages, recompense
lohs	1. loose; 2. (suffix) devoid of, lacking
lohs (f)	sow; lohsa (pl)
lohs (neu)	1. the portion that is received as a result of drawing lots; 2. a group of men chosen by the church to draw lots for ordination to the ministry
'lohva (glohbt) (ss)	to praise
'lokka (glokt)	1. to call an animal; 2. to draw or entice
'lossa (glost)	1. to allow; 2. to leave someone or something behind (contrast with "falossa")
luft (f)	air
lusht (f)	1. lust; 2. desire; lushta (pl)
'lushta (glusht)	1. to lust; 2. to desire
'lushtah`rei (f)	1. immorality; 2. covetousness
'lushtboah	lustful
'lushtboahkeit (f)	lustfulness

M

ma	1. one (pers. pronoun, nominative case); 2. short, unstressed form of "miah" (we)
ma (dative case)	a, an
'macha (gmacht)	1. to make; 2. to sound; 3. used extensively in idioms: "uf macha" (to open), "zu macha" (to close), "um macha" (to cut down)
macht (f)	power, authority, might
'maddah (m)	murderer; maddah (pl)
'maddah`rei (f)	murderous actions
maemm (f)	mother; maemma (pl)
'mandel (m)	robe; mandela (pl)
mann (m)	1. man; 2. husband; mennah (pl)
'mannich	many
'mans`kal (m)	man, male person; manskals (pl)
'mans`leit (pl)	men folk
matt	weak
maul (neu)	mouth; meilah (pl)
'maula (gmauld)	to argue
'maul`beahra	mulberry (adjective)
'mavvah (f)	wall; mavvahra (pl)
mawk	shall, may
'mawla (gmawla)	to grind
maws (f)	1. a measure; 2. temperance – frequently used in the idiomatic expression "ivvah di maws" (intemperately)
mawt (f)	1. servant maid; 2. hired maid;
mawda	(pl)
'mawwa	gaunt, emaciated

'mawwa (m)	stomach; mawwa (pl)
may	more
'maydel (neu)	girl; mayt (pl)
'mayna (gmaynd)	1. to mean; 2. to have an opinion; 3."sich mayna" (to be conceited)
'mayning (f)	1. meaning; 2. opinion; mayninga (pl)
'mayya (gmayt)	to mow
'mechta	might, would perhaps
'mechtich	strong, mighty
'meeklich	possible, capable of happening or being done
meel (f)	mill; meela (pl)
'meel-`shtay (m)	grinding wheel; meel-shtay (pl)
meet	tired
mei	my
meik (m)	mark; meiks (pl)
'meika (gmeikt)	to mark
meil (f)	mile; meil (pl)
meim (dative case)	my; meina (pl)
meind (f)	mind, memory
'meinda (gmeind)	1. to remember; 2. to mind, to care
'meishtah (m)	master; meishtahra (pl)
'meiya	tomorrow
'meiya (m)	morning; meiya (pl)
'meiya-`roht	morning red
'meiya-`shtann (f)	morning star
mensh (m)	human; mensha (pl)
'menshlich	pertaining to human reasoning
mensht	most
'messa (gmessa)	to measure
miah	we
miah (dative case)	me

54

mich	me
'middawk (f)	noon period
'middawk (neu)	noon meal
'midna/ mitt`na	contraction of "mitt eena" (with them)
'mikli (neu)	gnat, very small fly; miklen (pl)
'millich (f)	milk
'mint-`blansa (f)	mint plant; mint-blansa (pl)
misht (m)	1. manure; 2. you would have to
'missa	must
mist	would have to
mitt	with
'mitt-`dayl (neu)	similar fate or portion
'mitt-`dayla (mittgedayld)	to share
'mitt-`daylah (m)	1. one who shares the same fate; 2. one who shares; mitt-daylah (pl)
'mitt-`daylich	willing to share
'mitt-`deenah (m)	fellow servant; mitt-deenah (pl)
'mitt-`eahvah (m)	fellow heir; mitt-eahvah (pl)
'mitt-`eldishtah (m)	fellow elder; mitt-eldishti (pl)
'mitt-`gnecht (m)	fellow servant; mitt-gnechta (pl)
'mitt-`helfah (m)	helper; mitt-helfah (pl)
'mitt-`leida (mittglidda)	to sympathize
'mitt``na/ midna	contraction of "mitt eena" (with them)
'mitt-`nacht (f)	midnight
'mitt-`nannah	all together
'mitt-`shtreidah (m)	fellow soldier; mitt-shtreidah (pl)
mohl (neu)	one repetition, one time; mohl (pl)
moll	once, once upon a time
'moonet (m)	month; moonada (pl)
moot (f)	1. mood; 2. enthusiasm; 3. courage

'moshtaht (m)	mustard
'muddah (f)	mother; muddahra (pl)
'muddahs-`leib (f)	womb; muddahs-leivah (pl)
'mushtah (neu)	pattern; mushtahra (pl)
muss	must

N

na	contraction of "eena" (them)
na (dative case)	a, an
nacht (f)	night; necht (pl)
'nacht`mawl (neu)	religious communion meal
nachts	at night
'naddish	foolish
na`diahlich	1. carnal, not spiritual; 2. natural
na`duah (m)	1. temperament, disposition; 2. carnal nature
na`duaht	natured, having the disposition of
naett/nett	not
nah (m)	fool; narra (pl)
'nakkel-`loch (neu)	nail hole; nekkel-lechah (pl)
'nakkich	naked
'nakla (gnakeld)	to nail
'nannah	each other
nasht (m)	branch; nesht
nass	wet
natt (f)	North
'natt-`vest	northwest
nau	now
naus	toward an outer location
nay	no
nayksht	near; naychah, naykshtisht
'naymlich	namely

'nayva	located at the side
'nayvich	beside
'nayya (gnayt)	to sew
nee	never (not used alone)
'nee`mols	never, not even once
nei	1. toward an inner location; 2. new
'nei-`gmacht	1. made new, renewed; 2. built-in
nein	nine
'neina-`neintzich	ninety-nine
neind	ninth
'neintzich	ninety
'neiya	new
'neiyetz	nowhere
neksht	next
'nemma (gnumma)	to take
nesht (neu)	nest; neshtah (pl)
nett/ naett	not
nett (neu)	net; netts (pl)
'nevvel (m)	fog
'niddah	low
'nimmand	no one
'nimmi	no longer, no more
'nivvah	toward a location over there
nix	nothing
no	then
noch	1. yet; 2. after
'nocha`mohl	again
'nochbah (m)	neighbor; nochbahra (pl)
'nochbah`shaft (f)	neighborhood; nochbahshafta (pl)
'nochdi`hand	afterward
'nochmid`dawks	in the afternoon
nohch	after, behind, following

'nohch-`folya (nochkfolkt)* (ss) — to follow

'nohch-`folyah (m) — follower, disciple; noch-folyah (pl)

'nohch-`macha (nohchgmacht) — 1. to imitate, follow an example; 2. to follow

'nohch-`machah (m) — one who follows an example; nohch-machah (pl)

'nohdel (f) — needle; nohdla (pl)

'nohd`vendich — necessary

'nohma (m) — name; nayma (pl)

noht (f) — 1. necessity; 2. seam; nohda (pl)

nuff — toward a higher location

'nunnah — toward a lower location

'nunnah-be`zawling (f) — down payment; nunnah-betzawlinga (pl)

'nunnah-`lawda (nunnah-glawda) — to load down, burden

'nunnah-`ranna (nunnah-grand) — 1. to run down, become decrepit; 2. to run down, slander

O

oah (neu) — ear; oahra (pl)

oahm — poor

oahm (m) — arm; eahm (pl)

'oahma-`geld (neu) — funds for charity

'oahmoot (f) — 1. poverty; 2. pitiful condition

'oahrich — very

'oahrich (f) — ark; oahrichs (pl)

obsht (f) — fruit

offa (m) — oven; effa (pl)

`offen`boahring (f) — revelation; offenboahringa (pl)

oft — often

'oh`bayda (ohgebayda) — to worship

'oh`beeda (ohgebodda) — to offer

'oh`binna (ohgebunna) — to tie to a fixed object, to tether

'oh`bringa (ohgebrocht) — to incur

'oh`denka (ohgedenkt) — to estimate, esteem

'oh`denkes (neu) — a remembrance, souvenir

'oh`dreffa (ohgedroffa) — to meet

'ohdu (ohgedu) — to dress, put on

'oh`fang (m) — beginning; ohfanga (pl)

'oh`fanga (ohkfanga) — to begin

'ohften (m) — breath; ohften (pl)

'oh`gay (ohganga)* — 1. to concern, to be of importance to; 2. to ignite; 3. to light; 4. to happen or occur

'oh`glawwa (ohgeglawkt) (ss) — to accuse

'oh`globba (ohgeglobt) — to knock on a door, requesting entrance

'oh`gmohna (ohgegmohnd) — to remind

'oh`gnaymd — 1. well accepted; 2. highly honored

'oh`gukka (ohgegukt) — to look at

'oh`gunnish — envious

'oh`gunsht (m) — envy

'oh`halda/onhalda (ohkalda) — to continue

'oh`hayva (ohkohva) (ss) — to adhere to steadfastly

'oh`heicha (ohkeicht) — to listen to obediently

'oh`henka (ohkanka) — to hang onto

'oh`layya (ohglaykt) (ss) — to lay on – hands or clothes

'oh`lossa (ohglost) — 1. to pretend; 2. to leave on – a light, clothes, etc.

'oh`macha (ohgmacht) — 1. to light a fire or lamp; 2. to switch on a light; 3. to gain another`s favor

'oh`nemma (ohgnumma) — 1. to accept; 2. to adopt; 3. to endure patiently

'oh`rayya (ohgraykt) (ss) — to touch

59

'oh`roofa (ohgroofa) — to call upon

'oh`sayna (ohksenna) — to esteem, to rate

'oh`shikka (ohkshikt) — to act or behave

'oh`shpritza (ohkshpritzt) — to sprinkle an object with a liquid

'Ohshtah — Easter

'Ohshtah-`fesht (neu) — Passover feast

'Ohshtah-`lamm (neu) — sacrificial Passover lamb

'oh`shtekka (ohkshtekt/ohkshtokka) — 1. to light a fire or lamp; 2. to infect another with a contagious sickness

'ohvet (m) — evening; ohveda (pl)

'ohvet-`essa (neu) — evening meal; ohvet-essa (pl)

'ohvet-`roht — evening red

'oh`zeeya (ohgezowwa) (ss) — 1. to put on, to don; 2. to stretch over a frame 3. to draw moisture

oi (neu) — egg; oiyah (pl)

'on`halda/ohhalda (onkalda) — to continue

'oowah (f) — clock; oowahra (pl)

'opfah (neu) — sacrifice; opfahra (pl)

'opfah-`awldah (m) — altar used to sacrifice upon; opfah-awldahra (pl)

'opfah-`lamm (neu) — sacrificial lamb; opfah-lemmah (pl)

'opfahra (gopfaht) (ss) — to sacrifice

'ovva — located above

'ovva-`heah — from above

'ovvahrichkeit (f) — government; ovvahrichkeida (pl)

'ovvich — above

ox (m) — ox; oxa (pl)

P

'palma — palm (tree)

pa`tiklah — 1. particular; 2. especially

pawt (f) — path; pawda (pl)

peif (f)	1. whistle; 2. pipe used to smoke tobacco; 3. flute; peifa (pl)
'peifah (m)	one who whistles or plays a flute; peifah (pl)
'peif-`shpeelah (m)	flute player; peif-shpeelah (pl)
'pinklich	in great detail
'pishpahra (gepishpaht) (ss)	to whisper
poah	several
'poahbes	deliberately, on purpose
poahtsh (f)	porch; poahtsha (pl)
'preeshtah-`adning (f)	division of priests; preeshtah-adninga (pl)
'preeshtahshaft/-tum (f)	priesthood; preeshtahshafta/-tumma (pl)
'preeshtahtum/-shaft (neu)	preisthood; preeshtahtumma/-shafta (pl)
'preisa (geprissa)	to praise
'pshuldicha (pshuldicht)	to accuse
psuch (f)	visitors, company
'psucha (gepsucht)	to visit
'psuch-`leit (pl)	visitors, company
'psunna	disposed, minded
pund (f)	pound; pund (pl)
'punka (m)	point; punka (pl)

R

'rauda-`shtokk (m)	herb plant; rauda-shtekk (pl)
raus	out of
'rausha (grausht)	to make a rushing sound
'raus-`roofa (raus-groofa)	to call out of
'rawsa (grawst)	1. to move energetically; 2. to rave; 3. to rant or rage

'rawsich	1. energetic; 2. raging, uncontrolled
'rawva (grawbt) (ss)	to rob
'rawvah (m)	robber; rawvah (pl)
'rawvah`rei (f)	thievery
recht	correct, right
rechts	right (direction)
rei	in from outside
reich	rich
reich (neu)	kingdom; reicha (pl)
'reichheit (f)/-lichkeit	richness; reichheida (pl)
'reichlich	richly
'reichlichkeit (f)/-heit	richness; reichlichkeida (pl)
'reichtum (neu)	riches
'reida (gridda)	to ride
'reidah (m)	rider; reidahs (pl)
rein	pure
'reinicha (greinicht)	to cleanse, purify
'reiniching (f)	purification
'reinichkeit (f)	purity
'reisa (grissa)	to tear
'reiva (grivva) (ss)	1. to rub; 2. to tease
'renna (grend)	to shove or poke
'riahra (griaht) (ss)	to stir
'richta (gricht)	to judge
'richtah (m)	judge; richtah (pl)
'richtah-`dawk (m)	day of judgment; richtah-dawwa (pl)
'richtah-`shtool (m)	judgment seat; richtah-shteel (pl)
'richt-`haus (neu)	judgment hall; richt-heisah (pl)
'richtichkeit (f)	judgment
'richts-`blatz (m)	place of judgment; richts-bletz (pl)
rind (neu)	heifer; rinnah (pl)
'rishta (grisht)	to prepare

'risht-`dawk (m)	day of preparation; risht-dawwa (pl)
'rivvah	toward here
'rohda (grohda)	1. to advise; 2. to vote; 3. to counsel
rokk (m)	dress; rekk (pl)
'rolla (grold)	to roll
roo (f)	rest
roof (m)	call; roofa (pl)
'roofa (groofa)	to call
root (f)	rod, staff; rooda (pl)
'roowa (groot) (ss)	to rest
rosht (m)	rust
ruff	up from below
'ruich	quiet, restful
rumm	around
'rumm-`heah	in the general vicinity
'runnah	down from above
'runsel (m)	wrinkle; runsla (pl)

S

sach (f)	1. thing; 2. matter; sacha (pl)
'sadda	sort of
saft (f)	1. sap; 2. juice; safta (pl)
sakk (m)	sack; sekk (pl)
'sakk-`duch (neu)	sackcloth; sakk-dichah (pl)
'sakk-`glayt (neu)	garment of sackcloth; sakk-glaydah (pl)
'salba (ksalbt)	to anoint
'salba-`ayl (neu)	oil used for anointing
'salbing (f)	an anointing
sals (m)	salt
'salsich	salty
'samla (ksammeld)	to gather

63

'samling (f)	1. a gathering; 2. a collection; samlinga (pl)
samm	some
sand (m)	sand; sanda (pl)
'sanft`meedich	gentle, meek
'sanft`meedichkeit/sanftmoot (f)	meekness
'sanft`moot/sanftmeedichkeit (f)	meekness
'Satan (m)	Satan
satt	satiated, full
satt	kind, type; sadda (pl)
sau (f)	1. sow; 2. pig; sei (pl)
'sauda	south
'saufa (ksoffa)	1. to drink – used only of animals; 2. to drink an alcoholic beverage, usually to excess
'saufah`rei (f)	drinking of alcoholic beverages
saund	1. in good condition, sound; 2. doctrinally correct
saund (m)	sound, noise; saunds (pl)
saut (f)	the South
'saut-`vest	southwest
'sauvah	clean
'savvah	sour
'savvah-`dayk (m)	sourdough, leaven; savvah-dayka (pl)
'sawwa (ksawt) (ss)	to say
'sawwich	I say
say (m)	sea; sayya (pl)
sayf	safe, not dangerous
sayf (f)	1. soap; 2. safe, vault; sayfa (pl)
sayk (f)	1. sake, intent; 2. benefit; sayks (pl); 3. saw; sayya (pl)
'saykna (ksaykend)	to bless

sayl (f)	soul; sayla (pl)
'saylich	1. blessed; 2. saved
'saylichkeit (f)	salvation
saym	same
'sayna (ksenna)	to see
'sayya (ksaykt) (ss)	to saw
'sayya (ksayt)	to sow
'sayya (m)	blessing; sayya (pl)
'sayyah (m)	sower; sayyah (pl)
seahsht	first, preceding others
'secht`zay	sixteen
'sechtzich	sixty
'sedda	should
'sedla (kseddeld)	to settle
see	she, her
seel (m)	seal; seels (pl)
'seena (kseend)	to separate by passing through a sieve
sees	sweet
sei	his, hers, its
sei (gvest) (iv)	to be
'seida	made of silk
'sei-`heedah (m)	swineherd; sei-heedah (pl)
seik (f)	worry; seiya (pl)
seit (f)	side; seida/seits (pl)
'seiya (kseikt) (ss)	1. to ensure; 2. to take care of
se`layva	ever, even once
sell	that (demonstrative)
'sella	should, be supposed to
'selvaht	1. self; 2. alone
'setza (ksetzt)	1. to set or adjust; 2. to appoint; 3. to set one`s mind upon; 4. to set one`s confidence upon

sex	six
sext	sixth
'shadda (kshatt)	1. to matter; 2. to harm; 3. to scratch over the surface; 4. to scrape or rake
'shadda (m)	1. shadow; 2. shade; shadda (pl)
'shaffa (kshsaft)	to work
'shaffah (m)	worker; sheffah (pl)
shand (f)	1. disgrace, shame; 2. abomination; shanda (pl)
'shandlich	disgraceful, abominable
shatz (m)	apron; shatza (pl)
shauf	sharp
'shaufel (f)	shovel; shaufla (pl)
shaum (m)	foam
shawb (m)	1. moth; 2. fish scale; shawva (pl)
'shawda (m)	harm, damage; shawda
shawl (f)	1. peel, shell, crust; 2. outer covering; 3. shawl; shawla (pl)
'shawva (kshawbt) (ss)	1. to scrape off with a scraper; 2. to scale
shay	1. nice; 2. pretty; shennah, shensht
'shayfa (kshayft)	to shave
'shayheit (f)	prettiness
'sheahra (kshoahra) (ss)	to cut with a scissors
'shebba (kshebt)	to scoop or shovel
'sheeva (kshohva) (ss)	to push or shove
shein (m)	appearance, similitude
'sheina (ksheind)	1. to shine; 2. to appear
'sheiyah (f)	barn; sheiyahra (pl)
'shemma (kshemd)	1. to feel embarrassment or shame; 2. to feel shy
'shenka (kshenkt)	1. to give a gift; 2. to pardon

66

shiah	almost, nearly
shiah (f)	portion; shiahra (pl)
'shidla (kshiddeld)	to shake
shiff (neu)	ship; shiffah (pl)
'shiff-`gnecht (m)	sailor; shiff-gnechta (pl)
'shiff-`leit (pl)	the crew of a ship
'shiff-`meishtah (m)	shipmaster, captain; shiff-meishtahra (pl)
'shikka (kshikt)	to send
'shiklich	appropriate, suitable, proper
'shissel (f)	bowl; shisla (pl)
shkoll (m)	skull; shkols (pl)
'shkoll-`blatz (m)	the skull place
shlacht (f)	slaughter; shlachta (pl)
'shlachta (kshlacht)	to slaughter
'shlacht-`dawk (m)	day of slaughter; shlacht-dawwa (pl)
shlang (f)	snake; shlanga (pl)
'shlauwa (kshlauwa) (ss)	to hit
'shlawdra (kshlawdaht) (ss)	to slaughter
'shlayfa (kshlayft)	to drag
'shlayfah (m)	one who sleeps
'shlayfahrich	sleepy
shlecht	1. bad; 2. sick
'shleicha (kshlicha)*	to move stealthily
'shlichtich	1. crafty, dishonest; 2. secretly
'shlichtichkeit (f)	craftiness
'shliffah (m)	splinter; shliffahra (pl)
shlimm	terrible
'shlissel (m)	key; shlisla (pl)
'shlitz`oahrich	deceitful
shloh	slow
shlohf (m)	sleep

'shlohfa (kshlohfa)	to sleep
'shlohf-`haus (neu)	inn, hotel; shlohf-heisah (pl)
'shlohsa (kshlohsa)	to hail
'shlohsa (pl)	hailstones
'shlukka (kshlukt)	to swallow
'shmakka (kshmakt)	to smell
'shmakkich	smelly
shmatz (m)	pain; shmatza (pl)
'shmatza (kshmatzt)	to hurt
shmawl	narrow
'shmaychla (kshmaycheld)	to flatter or fawn upon; to seek favor
shmeaht	smart
'shmeisa (kshmissa)	to throw
shmiah (f)	1. salve; 2. any substance with a glutinous or viscous consistency; shmiahra (pl)
shmitt (m)	smith; shmidda (pl)
shmohk (m)	smoke
'shmohka (kshmohkt)	to smoke
shmukk (m)	adornment
shnay (m)	snow
'shneida (kshnidda)	to cut
shnell	quickly
'shnubb-`duch (neu)	handkercheif; shnubb-dichah (pl)
shohf (neu)	sheep; shohf (pl)
'shohf-`doah (neu)	(lit sheep door) door of a sheepfold; shohf-doahra (pl)
'shohf-`haut (f)	sheepskin; shohf-heit (pl)
'shohf-`heedah (m)	shepherd; shohf-heedah (pl)
'shohf-`shtall (m)	sheepfold; shohf-shtell (pl)
shohm (m)	shame, disgrace
shohs (f)	lap; shohsa (pl)

shoo (m)	shoe; shoo (pl)
'shoo-`bendel (m)	shoestring; shoe-bendel/-a (pl)
shool (f)	school; shoola (pl)
'shool-`meishtah (m)	schoolmaster; shool-meishtah (pl)
'shpalding (f)	schism; shpaldinga (pl)
shpatz (f)	sparrow; shpatza (pl)
shpautz (m)	spittle
'shpautza (kshpautzt)	to spit
'shpaydah	later
'shpeahra (kshpeaht) (ss)	1. to spare from death, pain, distress, expense, etc.; 2. to lend; 3. to have in excess
'shpeela (kshpeeld)	to play
shpees/shpiah (m)	spear; shpeesa (pl)
'shpeesa (kshpeest)	to spear
'shpeichah (m)	upstairs, second floor; shpeichahra (pl)
'shpeida (kshpeit)	to regret
shpeis (f)	food; shpeisa (pl)
'shpenda (kshpend)	to spend
shpiah/shpees (m)	spear; shpiahs
'shpikkel (m)	mirror; shpikla (pl)
'shpitza (m)	point; shpitza (pl)
'shpoahra (kshpoaht) (ss)	to use sparingly or frugally
'shpodda (kshpott)	to mock
'shpoddah (m)	mocker; shpeddah (pl)
shpoht	late
'shpoht-yoah (neu)	fall, autumn
shprau (neu)	chaff
'shprich-vatt (neu)	proverb; shprich-vadda (pl)
'shpringa (kshprunga)*	to run
'shpritza (kshpritzt)	to sprinkle or spray
shprohch (f)	language; shprohcha (pl)

'shreinah (m)	carpenter; shreinah (pl)
'shreiva (kshrivva) (ss)	to write
'shreklich	terrifying, awful
Shrift (f)	Scriptures; Shrifta (pl)
'shrift-ge`leahrah (m)	scribe; shrift-geleahrah (pl)
'shtadda (kshtatt)/shtarra	to stir
shtaend (m)	platform or stand; shtaends (pl)
shtall (m)	1. stall; 2. building that shelters one kind of animal; 3. section of barn used for storing hay or grain, etc.; shtell (pl)
'shtamba (kshtambt)	to stamp
shtamm (m)	1. family, race; 2. trunk of a tree; 3. stem; shtemm (pl)
'shtand`haftich	steadfast
'shtand`haftichkeit (f)	steadfastness
shtann (f)	1. star; 2. forehead; shtanna (pl)
'shtarra (kshtatt)/shtadda	to stir
shtatt (f)	town; shtett (pl)
'shtatt-`richtah (m)	magistrate; shtatt-richtah (pl)
'shtatza (kshtatzt)*	to stumble
'shtauva (kshtauva)*/shteahva	to die
shtawb (m)	dust
shtay (kshtanna) (iv)	to stand
shtay (m)	stone; shtay (pl)
shtayk (f)	stairs; shtayya (pl)
shtayla (kshtohla)	to steal
'shtaylah (m)	thief; shtaylah (pl)
'shtaylah`rei (f)	thievery
'shtaynich	1. stony; 2. made of stone
'shtaynicha (kshtaynicht)	to stone
'shtay-`tablet (neu)	tablet of stone; shtay-tablets (pl)

'shteahblich	subject to death, mortal
'shteahra (kshteaht) (ss)	to start
'shteahva (kshteahva)*/shtauva	to die
'shtecha (kshtocha)	1. to prick or pierce; 2. to sting
'shtechah (m)	1. stinger; 2. a sharp pointed instrument that pierces; shtechah (pl)
'shteddel/shtedli (neu)	town, village; shtedlen (pl)
'shtedli/shteddel (neu)	town, village; shtedlen (pl)
'shteef-`maemm (f)	stepmother; shteef-maemma (pl)
'shteibahra (kshteibaht) (ss)	1. to brace; 2. to resist
'shteibahrich	stubborn, obstinate
shteif	stiff
shteik	1. fast; 2. strong
'shtekka (kshtokka)	1. to insert; 2. to stick, adhere
'shtekka (m)	stick; shtekka (pl)
'shtekli (neu)	1. small plant; 2. small stick; shteklen (pl)
'shtella (kshteld)	1. to set or place an object; 2. to appoint a date or time
'shtenda (kshtend)	to bear or suffer
'shtengel (m)	1. stem; 2. rhubarb; shtengel (pl)
'shtiah-`boaht (neu)	(lit. steering board) rudder; shtiah-beaht (pl)
'shtiah-`mann (m)	pilot; shtiah-mennah (pl)
shtikk (neu)	1. piece; shtikkah (pl); 2. a small distance
'shtikka (kshtikt, kshtokka)	1. to stick, adhere; 2. to persevere
shtill	still, quiet
shtimm (f)	voice; shtimma (pl)
'shtinka (kshtunka)	to stink
shtoah (m)	store; shtoahra (pl)
'shtoah-`haus (neu)	storehouse; shtoah-heisah (pl)

'shtoahm (m)	storm; shtoahms (pl)
'shtoah`mich	stormy
'shtoahri (f)	story; shtoahris (pl)
'shtobba (kshtobt)	to stop
'shtohsa (kshtohsa)	1. to cast or throw; 2. to thrust; 3. to take offense
shtokk (m)	1. plant; 2. walking stick; shtekk (pl)
'shtolbah-`blakk (m)	stumbling block; shtolbah-blaks (pl)
'shtolbahra (kshtolbaht)* (ss)	to stumble
'shtolbah-`shtay (m)	stumblingstone; shtolbah-shtay (pl)
shtols	1. proud; 2. stubborn
shtool (m)	chair; shteel (pl)
shtraych (m)	1. stripe or streak; 2. stroke or blow; 3. stroke, attack of paralysis; 4. a period of time; shtraych (pl)
'shtreida (kshtridda)	to battle
shtreit (m)	battle; shtreida (pl)
shtreng	strict
'shtrichli (neu)	1. a small stroke; 2. a small caress; shtrichlen (pl)
shtrikk (m)	rope; shtrikk (pl)
shtrohf (m)	punishment; shtrohfa (pl)
'shtrohfa (kshtrohft)	to punish
'shtrohf-`dawk (m)	day of punishment; shtrohf-dawwa (pl)
'shtrohf-`zeit (f)	time of punishment; shtrohf-zeida (pl)
shtrohs (f)	street; shtrohsa (pl)
'shtrohsa-`leng (f)	length of a street; shtrohsa-leng (pl)
'shtrohs-`ekk (neu)	corner of a street; shtrohs-ekka/-ah (pl)
'shtroiya (kshtroit)	1. to scatter; 2. to spread bedding for livestock
shtubb (f)	room; shtubba (pl)
shtund (f)	hour; shtund/-a (pl)

shuah	sure
shuld (f)	1. fault, blame; 2. debt; shulda (pl)
'shuldah (m)	shoulder; shuldra (pl)
'shuldich	1. at fault, blameworthy; 2. indebted to, under obligation
'shuldichkeit (f)	obligation; shuldichkeida (pl)
'shuld`lohs	blameless
shund	already
shunsht	1. otherwise; 2. in addition, else
shvach	weak; shvechah, shvechsht
'shvach`heit (f)	weakness; shvachheida (pl)
'shvadda-`shnitt (m)	1. edge of a sword; 2. cut made by a sword
shvans (m)	tail; shvens (pl)
shvatt (neu)	sword; shvadda (pl)
shvatz	black
shveah	heavy
'shveahra (kshvoahra) (ss)	1. to vow; make an oath; 2. to swear
'shveshtah (f)	sister; shveshtra (pl)
'shvetza (kshvetzt)	to talk
'shvetzah (m)	talker; shvetzah (pl)
'shvevvel (neu)	sulphur
'shviah-`dochtah (f)	daughter-in-law; shviah-dochtahra (pl)
'shviah-`muddah (f)	mother-in-law; shviah-muddahra (pl)
'shvimma (kshvumma)*	to swim
shvitz (m)	sweat
si	they, them
sich	self (reflexive)
'sichel (f)	1. sickle; 2. blade or shoot on a plant; sichla (pl)
'siddah	since
'siffah (m)	alcoholic; siffah (pl)

'sifta (ksift)	to sift
'silvah	silver
'silvah-`shmitt (m)	silversmith; silvah-shmitt (pl)
sind (f)	sin, transgression; sinda (pl)
'sindah (m)	sinner; sindah (pl)
'sind`floot (f)	(lit. sin flood) the flood God used to destroy the inhabitants of the earth
'sindfol	sinful
'sindicha (ksindicht)	to sin
'sindlich	sinful
'sind-`opfah (neu)	offering for sin; sind-opfahra (pl)
'singa (ksunga)	to sing
'singah (m)	singer; singah (pl)
sinn	are
sitz (m)	seat; sitza (pl)
'sivva	seven
'sivveda	the seventh one
'sivvet	seventh
'sivvetzich	seventy
so	1. so; 2. therefore
'sobbah (neu)	supper; sobbahs (pl)
'soddich/sohwich	suchlike
'soffahra (ksoffaht) (ss)	to suffer
'sohbah	sober
sohm (m)	seam; sohma (pl)
'sohma (m)	seed; sohma (pl)
sohn (m)	son; sayna (pl)
'sohwich/soddich	suchlike
soll	shall, should
'sooda (ksoot)	1. to suit; 2. to please
'sucha (ksucht)	to seek
'summah (m)	summer; summahra (pl)

sunn (f)	sun; sunna (pl)
'sunn-`unnah	sundown

T

'taena (getaend)	to tan
'taenah (m)	tanner; taenah (pl)
'tavvah (m)	tower; tavvahs (pl)
'tax-`dish (m)	(lit. tax table) tax collector`s desk; taxdisha (pl)
'tax-`ei`nemmah (m)	tax collector; tax-einemmah (pl)
'tayklich	daily
'teetshah (m)	teacher; teetshahs (pl)
'tempel (m)	temple; tempels (pl)
'tempel-`box (f)	(lit. temple box) treasury; tempel-boxa (pl)
'tempel-`broht (neu)	(lit. temple bread) ceremonial shew-bread
'tempel-`fesht (neu)	(lit. temple feast) feast of dedication; tempel-feshta (pl)
'tent-`tempel (m)	(lit. tent temple) ceremonial tabernacle; tent-tempels (pl)
'Teshtament (neu)	Testament; Teshtamenta/-ah (pl)
'tshaynsha (getshaynsht)	to change
tsheah (m)	jar; tsheahs (pl)
'tsheahtsha (getsheahtsht)	to charge
'tshumba (getshumbt)*	to jump

U

'uah`sach (f)	reason, cause; uahsacha (pl)
uf	1. on, upon; 2. open; 3. up; 4. (separable prefix) on, open, up
'uffana (neu)	a wide unobstructed space

`uffa`shtaying (f)	resurrection; uffashtayinga (pl)
'uf lichta (ufglicht)	to light up
'uf mundahra (ufgmundaht) (ss)	to encourage
'uf richtich	upright, honest
'uf richtichkeit (f)	uprightness, honesty
'uf rohma (ufgrohmd)	to tidy up
'uf ruah (m)	tumult; ufruahra (pl)
um	1. (separable prefix) down, dead, around; 2. approximately, about; 3. around
'um`bringa (umgebrocht)	to kill
'um`kumma (umkumma)*	to die
'um`mechtich	faint, unconscious
'um`meeklich	impossible
'um`shmeisa (umkshmissa)	1. to upset, capsize; 2. to overthrow
un	and
'una	contraction of "un en" (and a)
'un`adlich	lawless
'un`adning (f)	disorder
'un`aydich	unnecessary
'un`aynich	not in unity, in disagreement
'un`aynichkeit (f)	disunity; unaynichkeida (pl)
`unbam`hatzich	merciless
`unbe`greiflich	astonishing, incomprehensible
'unbe`kand	unknown
`unbe`kimmaht	unconcerned
`unbe`shneiding (f)	uncircumcision
`unbe`shnidda	uncircumcised
'un`dankboah	unthankful
'un`eahlich	dishonest
`unfa`genglich	imperishable
'unfa`hoft	unexpected

'unfa`seikt	1. not taken care of; 2. unaccomplished
`unfa`shtendlich	1. without understanding; 2. intemperate
`unfa`shtendlichkeit (f)	1. state of being without understanding; 2. intemperance
'un`fruchtboah	unfruitful
'unge`boahra	unborn
'unge`glayt	unclothed
'unge`horsam	disobedient
'un`geishtlich	unholy
'unge`recht/-ich	unrighteous
'unge`rechtichkeit (f)	unrighteousness
'un`getlich	ungodly
'un`getlichkeit (f)	ungodliness
'un`gland	1. unlearned; 2. lacking in social graces
'un`glawva (m)	unbelief
'un`glawvich	unbelieving
'Un`greeyish	not of Greek nationality
'un`ksavvaht	unleavened
'un`ksheit	1. not sensible; 2. risky, foolhardy
'un`kshikt	1. improper; 2. not talented
'un`kshrunka	not preshrunk
'unna	located down below; at the bottom
'unnah	1. under; 2. (pref) under
'unnah-`hauptmann (m)	centurion; unnah-hauptmennah (pl)
'unnah-`nemma (unnah-gnumma)	to undertake, to attempt
'unnahs-`evvahsht	upside down
'unnah`shitt (m)	difference; unnahshidda (pl)
'unnah`shidlich	1. distinguishable; 2. various; 3. changeable

'unnah-`sucha (unnah-ksucht)	to examine, search out
'unni	without
'unnich	under
'unrein	impure
'un`reinichkeit (f)	impurity
'unroo (f)	unrest
'un`ruich	restless
uns	us
'unsah	our
'un`sauvah	unclean
'un`shiklich	improper
'un`shprechlich	too magnificent to express in words
`unshtandhaftich	unstable
'un`shtrayflich	blameless
'un`shuldich	innocent
'un`shuldichkeit (f)	innocence
'un`veahdich	unworthy
'un`villich	unwilling, reluctant
'un`voahret (f)	untruth, falsehood
'un`zucht (f)	licentiousness

V

'vadda (vadda)*	to become
'vakkah	awake
'val`fish (m)	whale; valfish (pl)
'vammes (m)	coat; vemmes (pl)
vand (f)	wall; vanda (pl)
vann	1. when; 2. if
vann	one (pronoun); vans (pl)
'vanna (gvand)	to warn
vann-`evvah	whenever
'vanning (f)	warning; vanninga (pl)

78

vass	1. what; 2. (relative pronoun) that, which, who
'vassah (neu)	1. water; 2. a body of water; vassahra (pl)
'vassah-`loch (neu)	1. watering hole; 2. mud puddle; vassah-lechah (pl)
'vassah-`shpring (f)	spring of water; vassah-shpringa (pl)
'vassah-`sucht (f)	dropsy
vass-`evvah	whatever
vatsh (f)	1. the period during which a guard is on duty; 2. watch, timepiece; vatsha (pl)
'vatsha (gvatsht)	to watch
vatt (neu)	word; vadda (pl)
'vatzel (f)	root; vatzla (pl)
'vauwa (m)	large wagon; vauwa (pl)
'vaxa (gvaxa)*	to grow
vay	painful, sore
vay (f)	woe; vayya (pl)
vayk (m)	1. way; 2. road; vayya (pl)
vayks	ways – a suffix of adverbs; ex. "shtikk vayks" (partways)
'vaysa (neu)	unnecessary fuss or display
vayt (f)	pasture; vayda (pl)
'vaytza (m)	wheat
'vayyich-`hatzich	softhearted
veah	who
veah-`evvah	whoever
'veah`lohs	nonresistant
'veahma (gveahmd)	1. to warm; 2. to worm
'veahra	would be
'veahra (gveaht) (ss)	to show reluctance
'veahra (gvoahra) (ss)	to wear

veaht (f)	worth, value
'veahtfol	worthy
'veahtfollich	worthwhile
'vedda	would want
'veddah	contacting, against
'veddah (neu)	weather
'veddah-`laych (m)	lightning; veddah-laycha (pl)
'veddah-`laycha (veddah-glaycht)	to flash lightning
'veecha (m)	wick; veecha (pl)
veesht	bad, evil
'veeshtahlich	wickedly
veetz (neu)	weeds
vei	why (preface to a remark)
vei (m)	wine
veib (neu)	woman; veivah (pl)
'veibs`mensh (neu)	female person; veibsleit (pl)
'vei-`drohk (m)	wine vat; vei-drayk (pl)
'vei-`goahra (m)	vineyard; vei-goahra (pl)
'veiklich	truly
veil	1. while; 2. because; 3. a little while
'veina (gveind)	to weep
'vei-`press (f)	winepress; vei-presses (pl)
veis	white
veis (f)	tune; veisa (pl)
'veisa (gvissa)	to show
'vei-`sakk (m)	wineskin; vei-sekk (pl)
'vei-`saufah (m)	wine drinker; vei-saufah (pl)
'vei-`shtokk (m)	grapevine; vei-shtekk (pl)
'veis`heit (f)	wisdom
'veising (f)	revelation; veisinga (pl)
'veisla (gveiseld)	to whitewash
veit	far

vekk	away
'vekka (gvekt)	to wake up
veld (f)	world; velda (pl)
'veldlich	worldly
velk	wilted
vell	well (preface to a remark)
vell (f)	wave of water; vella (pl)
'vella (vella) (iv)	to want
vels	which one
vemm	whom
vemm sei	whose
'vennich	1. a little; 2. few
verk (neu)	work, accomplishment; verka (pl)
vesh (f)	laundry
'vesha (gvesha)	to wash
'vesh-`shissel (f)	washbowl; vesh-shisla (pl)
vest	west
'vexel (m)	1. monetary change; 2. trade
'veyya/veyyich	about, concerning
'veyyich/veyya	about, concerning
vi	1. how; 2. as, like; 3. than
'vichtich	weighty, important
'viddah	1. again; 2. against, opposed to
'viddah`bat (neu)	argument, verbal opposition
'viddah`bat-`haldah (m)	a person given to arguing; viddahbat-haldah (pl)
'viddah-`christ	antichrist; viddah-chrishta (pl)
'viddah-ge`boahra	born again
'viddah-`shtand (m)	defense, opposition
'viddah-`shtreit (m)	opposition
'vikla (gvikkeld)	to wrap
vild	wild

'vildahnis (f)	wilderness; vildahnissa (pl)
'villa (m)	1. the power to make choices; 2. desire; 3. document directing a person`s property distribution after his death; villa (pl)
'villich	willing
'villichlich	willingly
vind (m)	wind; vinda (pl)
'vindah (m)	winter; vindra (pl)
'vindla-`duch (neu)	diaper cloth; vindla-dichah (pl)
'vind-`shtoahm (m)	windstorm; vind-shteahm (pl)
'vinsha (gvinsht)/vodda	to wish
vissa (gvist) (iv)	to know – information or facts
'vissaheit (f)	knowledge
vista	would know
'vitt-`fraw (f)	widow; vitt-veivah (pl)
'vitt-`veib (neu)	widow; vitt-veivah (pl)
vo	1. where; 2. (relative pronoun) that, which, who
voah	true
voah	was
voah`haftich	1. truly, certainly; 2. genuine; 3. faithful
'voah`heit/voahret (f)	truth
'voahlich	truly
voahm	warm; veahmah, veahmsht
voahm (m)	worm; veahm (pl)
'voahra	were
'voahra (gvoaht) (iv)	to wait
'voahret/voahheit (f)	truth
'voahrich	I was
'voah-`sawwa (voah-ksawt) (ss)	to tell a fortune

'voah-`sawwah (m)	fortune teller; voah-sawwah (pl)
voch (f)	week; vocha (pl)
'vodda (gvott)/vinsha	to wish
vo-`evvah	wherever
'voh`heah	why, wherefore
vohk (f)	scales; vohwwa (pl)
'vohl-`kfalla (neu)	good will, pleasure
'voh`lusht	1. fleshly pleasure; 2. fleshly desire; vohlushta (pl)
'vohning (f)	dwelling, abode; vohninga (pl)
volf (m)	wolf; velf (pl)
volk (f)	cloud; volka (pl)
'volkich	cloudy
voll	of course, certainly
'voona (gvoond)	to dwell
'voon-`blatz (m)	dwelling place; voon-bletz (pl)
vull (f)	wool
'vundah/vunnah (m)	marvel, wonder; vundah (pl)
'vundah`boah	amazing
`vundah`boahlich	amazingly
'vunnah/vundah (m)	marvel, wonder; vunnahs (pl)
'vunnahra (gvunnaht) (ss)	to wonder

Y

yacht (f)	noise; yachta (pl)
'yachtich	noisy
'yammahlich	lamentable, wretched
'yammahra (gyammaht) (ss)	to lament, to groan
yau	yes
'yawwa (gyawkt) (ss)	to chase
'yaydah	each
'yeahs-`dawk (m)	birthday; yeahs-dawwa (pl)

'Yiddish	Jewish
'yingah (m)	disciple; yingah (pl)
yo	1. yes; only used when contradicting a negative statement; 2. by all means; be very careful
yoah (neu)	year; yoahra (pl)
yoaht (m)	yard – 36 inches; yoaht (pl)
yoch (neu)	yoke; yocha (pl)
'yoosa (gyoost)	to use
'Yudda-`council (f)	Jewish council
'Yudda-`gmay (pl)	Jewish church; Yudda-gmayna (pl)
yung	young; yingah, yingsht
yusht	only, just
Yutt (m)	Jew; Yudda (pl)

Z

'zahbahrah (m)	sorcerer; zahbahrah (pl)
'zammah	together
zank (m)	strife, arguing
'zanka (gezankt)	to scold
zann (m)	anger
'zannich	furious
'zarra (gezatt)	1. to tease; 2. to argue
'zaufa (gezauft)	to bicker
'zaycha (m)	1. miracle or special sign; 2. pointer of a clock or meter; zaycha (pl)
'zaycha-`shaffah (m)	worker of miracles; zaycha-sheffah (pl)
zayl	will, shall
'zayla (gezayld)	to count
'zebba (gezebt)	to braid
'zeeya (gezohwa) (ss)	1. to pull; 2. to move to another residence

zeit (f)	time; zeida (pl)
'zeiya (gezeigt) (ss)	1. to witness or testify; 2. to beget
'zeiya (m)	1. witness; 2. news; zeiya (pl)
'zeiyah (m)	one who testifies; zeiyah (pl)
'zeyya	ten
'zeyya (m)	toe; zeyya (pl)
'zeyyadel (neu)	one tenth
'zeyyet	tenth
'ziddahra (geziddaht) (ss)	to shiver or tremble
zoh (m)	tooth; zay (pl)
zohm	tame
zohm (m)	bridle; zaym (pl)
'zohma (gezohmd)	to tame
zrikk	1. toward a former place or state; 2. return or reply
'zrikk-be`zawlah (m)	1. one who revenges; 2. one who pays back; zrikk-bezawlah (pl)
'zrikk-`shtohsa (zrikk-kshtohsa)	1. to cast back; 2. to reject
zu	1. to; 2. too, in excess; 3. closed
'zu-`dekka (zu-gedekt)	to cover
zu`fridda	content
'zumma	contraction of "zu en" (to a)
zung (f)	1. tongue; 2. language; zunga (pl)
'zvansich	twenty
zvay	two
zvayk	1. tidy; 2. in order; 3. onward, along; ex. "zvayk kumma" (get along)
'zvay-`ksichtich	two-faced, deceitful
'zvay-`shneidich	having two cutting edges
'zveicha (gezveicht)	to graft
'zveifla (gezveifeld)	to doubt
zvelf	twelve

zvelft	twelfth
zvett	the second one
'zvilling (m)	twin; zvilling (pl)
'zvinga (gezvunga)	to compel
'zvisha	between
'zvishich	between

ENGLISH to DEITSH

A

a, an	en/na (dative case)
abominable	greilich
abomination	shand
about it	diveyya
about, concerning	veyya/veyyich
above	ovvich
accept	ohnemma
accountable	fa'andvadlich
accusation	glawk
accuse	faglawwa/fashuldicha/ohglawwa/ pshuldicha
accustom to	gvayna
acre	akkah
across	drivvah
act, behave	ohshikka
adhere to	ohhayva/shtikka
adjust	setza
admonish	famohna
admonition	famohning
adornment	shmukk
adulterer	aybrechah
adultery	aybruch
adultery, to commit	aybrecha
advise	rohda
after	noch
after all	doch
afternoon, in the	nochmiddawks
afterward	dinohch/nochdihand
again	ivvah/nochamohl/viddah
age (n)	eld

aged	eldlich
agree	fa'aynicha/eiseida/eishtimma
agreed	aynich/difoah
ahead of	fanna-heah
air	luft
alcoholic (n)	siffah
alive	levendich/levvich
all	allem/awl
allow	alawva/lossa
allowed	daufa
allowed, would be	deift
almighty	almechtich/awlmechtich
almost	fasht
alms	almohsa
alone	laynich/selvaht
already	shund
also	aw
altar	awldah/opfah-awldah
always	immah
amazing	vundahboah
amazingly	vundahboahlich
ambassador	botshaftah
an	en
anchor (n)	enkah
anchor hook	enkah-hohka
and	un
angel	engel
anger	zann
angry	bays
animal	diah
annoyed	ausfix
anoint	salba

anointing (n)	salbing
another one	anres
answer (v)	andvadda/fa'andvadda
antichrist	viddah-chrisht
anxiety	angsht
anxious, worried	engshtlich
any	ennich
apostasy	abfall
apostle	aposhtel
appear, seem	sheina
appearance, similitude	shein
appoint	setza
appointed	ksetzt
appropriate	shiklich
approved	kfellich
approximately	um
apron	shatz
archangel	hohch-engel
are	sinn
area, location	gaygend
argue	maula/zadda
arguing, habitual	gezahh
argumentative person	viddahbat-haldah
ark of the covenant	bundes-lawt
arm (n)	oahm
armor	greeks-ksha
army captain	greeks-hauptman
around	rumm/um
ashes	esh
ask	frohwa
assemble in meeting	fasamla
assistance	hilf

associate with	eigay
assuredly	fashuah
astonish	fashtauna/favunnahra
at	an/anna
at (pref)	anna
at home	dihaym
at night	nachts
at that time	ivvah demm
at the side	nayvah
at the top	ovva
at times	als
attain	alanga
attempt (v)	broviahra, fasucha
authority	macht
autumn	shpoht-yoah
awake (adj)	vakkah
awaken	vekka
away	fatt/vekk
away from here	difunn
ax	ax
axle	ax

B

baby	bobli
back (n)	bukkel
back, at the	hinna
back, the farthest to	hinnahsht
backward	hinnahsich
bad	shlecht
bake	bakka
baptism	dawf
baptize	dawfa

baptizing, act of	gedawf
barley	geahsht
barley bread	geahsht-broht
barn	sheiyah
basket	koahb
basket full	koahb-foll
battle (n)	shtreit
battle (v)	shtreida
be	sei
beam (of wood)	balka
bear (n)	beah
bear, suffer	shtenda
beast that blasphemes	leshtah-diah
beat (v)	globba
beat up (v)	faglobba/fashlauwa
because	veil
because of it	dideich
become	vadda
bed (n)	bett
bed of blankets on floor	bodda-nesht
before	difoah/eb/fa
beg	bedla
beget	zeiya
begin	ohfanga
beginning	ohfang
behead	kebba
behind (adv)	hinnich
belief	glawva
believe	glawva
bell	bell
beloved	beleebt/geleebt/leeb/leevich
belt (n)	belt

bench (n)	bank
bend (v)	beeya
bend over	ivvah-beeya
benefit (n)	sayk
benefit (v)	badda
beside	nayvich
best	besht
betray	farohda
betrayed	bedrohwa
better	bessah
between	kshvissich/zvisha/zvishich
beverage	drinkes
beware of	heeda
bicker	zaufa
bid (v)	beeda/bidda
big	grohs
bird	fokkel
birthday	yeahs-dawk
bishop	bishof
bit (bridle)	gebiss
bite (v)	beisa
bitter	biddah
bitter herbs	biddahgreidah
bitter, to become	fabiddahra
bitterly	biddahlich
black	shvatz
blameless	shuldlohs/unshtrayflich
blameworthy	shuldich
blaspheme	leshtahra/faleshtahra
blasphemer	leshtahrah
blaspheming, habitual	geleshtah
bleed	blooda

bleeding sickness	bloots-granket
bless	saykna
blessed	saylich
blessing	sayya
blind (adj)	blind
blind (v)	fablenna
blindness	blindheit
blink of an eye	awwa-blikk
blood	bloot
bloodstream	blood-shtrayma
blow (n)	hakk
blow (v)	blohsa
blow away	fablohsa
blower	blohsah
blue	bloh
boat	boat
bodily	leiblich
body	leib
boil (wound)	kshveah
bone	gnocha
book	buch
Book of life	layves-buch
booklet	bichli
bored with	laydich
born	geboahra
born again	viddah-geboahra
borrow	layna
bossy	foahvitzich
bother (v)	baddahra/blohwa
bother (n)	baddah/blohk
bothersome	blohwich
bottle	boddel

bottom, at the	unna
boulder	felsa
bow (n)	bow
bowl (n)	bowl/shissel
box (n)	box
boy	boo
boy, little	boovli
brace (v)	shteibahra
brag (v)	braekka
bragging, habitual	gebraekk
braid (v)	zebba
branch (n)	nasht
brass	brass
bread	broht
bread of heaven	Himmel's broht
break (v)	brecha/fabrecha
break off	abbrecha
break out	ausbrecha
breast	brusht
breastplate	brusht-playt
breath	ohften
bride	hochtzich-maydel
bridegroom	hochtzeidah/hochtzich-mann
bridle (n)	zohm
bright (light)	hell
brightness	glantz
bring	bringa
broom	baysa
brother	broodah
brotherly	breedahlich
build	bauwa
building	gebei

built-in	nei-gmacht
bull	bull
bundle	bundel
burden (n)	lasht
burn	brenna/fabrenna
burnt offering	brand-opfah
burst (v)	fablohsa/fabosta
bury	fagrawva
bushel	bushel
bushel basket	bushel-koahb
but	avvah
buy (v)	kawfa
by	bei

C

calculate	fikkahra
calf	hamli/kalb
call (n)	roof
call (v)	roof
call an animal	lokka
call out	ausroofa
call out of	raus-roofa
call upon	ohroofa
called	groofa
calling (n)	beroof
camel	kamayl
can	kann
captain	hauptmann
care about	drumm gevva
care for, tend	faseiya/heeda
caregiver	heedah
caress (n)	shtrichli

carnal	nadiahlich
carpenter	shreinah
carry	drawwa
carry out	ausdrawwa
cast a spell	fahexa
cast back	zrikk-shtohsa
cat	katz
catch (v)	fanga
cause (n)	uahsach
cause to stumble or err	fashtatza
cave	felsa-loch
cent	cent
centurion	unnahhauptmann
ceremonial hut of branches	lawb-haus
certain ones	dayl
chaff	shprau
chain (n)	kett
chair	shtool
change (money)	vexel
change (v)	fa'ennahra/tshaynsha
change one's appearance	fashtella
changeable	unnahshidlich
charge, set a price	tsheahtsha
chase (v)	dreiva/yawwa/fayawwa
chastity	keishheit
chest (furniture)	kashta
chick	beebli
child	kind
childish	kindish
children of thunder	Dimmels-kinnah
choice	avayling
choose	avayla

choose or call ahead of time	foahroofa
chop off	abhakka
Christ	Chrishtus
Christian	Grishta-mensh
Christ-like	Grishtlich
church group	gmay
church house	gmay-haus
church service	gmay
circumcise	beshneida
circumcision	beshneiding
city	shtatt
clarify	fakleahra
clean (adj)	sauvah
clean (v)	butza
clear (adj)	kliah
clearness	gloahheit
clock	oowah
closed (adj)	zu
cloth	duch
clothe	glayda
cloud (n)	volk
cloudy	volkich
clump	glumba
clump of bushes	hekka-putsha
coal	kohl
coat (garment)	ivvah-hemm/vammes
coat, heavy (garment)	ivvah-rokk
cob	kolva
coffin	lawt
coin (n)	grosha
cold	kald
collar (n)	band

collection	samling
colt	hutsh
comb (v)	kemma
come	kumma
comfort (n)	drohsht
comfort (v)	drohshta
comforter	drayshtah
command (n)	addah/gebott
communion meal	nachtmohl
community	gaygend
compel	zvinga
complain	glawwa
complain about	faglawwa
complaint	glawk
completely	goah
comprehend	begreifa
comprehension	fashtendnis
comrade	kumrawt
concede to	eigevva
conceited	grohs-feelich
concern, to be of	ohgay
concern, to take	bekimmahra
condemn	fadamma
condemnation	fadamnis
conduct (n)	layves-lawf
confess	bekenna
confession	bekendnis
confidence	fadrauwa/fadrohsht
confine	eishpadda
confuse	fahudla/fashtatza
conquer	ivvah-vinna
conscience	gvissa

consequently (conjunction)	dann
considerably, fairly	adlich
consume	fazeahra
consuming (adj)	fazeahrich
contacting, against	veddah
content (adj)	zufridda
continue	ohhalda/onhalda
contrary to one's will	ingeyya
convulsions	gichtahra
cook (v)	kocha
cool (adj)	keel
cool (v)	keela
cool off	abkeela
copper	kubbah
coppersmith	kubbah-shmitt
copy by writing (v)	abshreiva
corn, ear of	kolva
corner (n)	ekk
corner of a street	shtrohs-ekk
corner stone	ekk-shtay
cost (v)	koshta
costly	koshtboah
count (v)	zayla
courage	moot
courtyard	haus-hohf
covenant	bund
cover (v)	dekka/zu-dekka
cover over	ivvah-dekka
coveteousness	geitz/lushtahrei
covetous	geitzich
covetous of honor	eahgeitzich
craftiness	shlichtichkeit

crafty	shlichtich
crawl (v)	gradla
creation	ksheft
creek	grikk
creep stealthily	shleicha
crew of a ship	shiff-leit
cripple (n)	gribbel
cripple (v)	fagribla/gribla
crippled ones	fagribbelda
crock	haffa
crooked	grumm
cross (n)	greitz
crow (n)	grabb
crow (v)	grayya
crowd (n)	crowd
crown (n)	krohn
crown (v)	krohna
crown of life	layves-krohn
crucify	greitzicha
crumb	brokka/grimmel
crutch	grikk
cry (v)	brilla
crying (n)	brilles
crystal glass	crystal-glaws
cup	kobli
curious	gvunnahrich
curry favor	ohmacha
curse (n)	fluch
curse (v)	flucha
curse at	faflucha
curtain	curtain
custom	gebrauch

101

customarily	gvaynlich
cut (v)	shneida
cut made by a sword	shvadda-shnitt
cut off	abshneida
cut with a scissors	sheahra

D

daily	tayklich
damage (n)	shawda
damage (v)	fadauva/fadeahva
dance (v)	dansa
danger	kfoah
dangerous	kfeahlich
dare (verb, intransitive)	drauwa
dark	dunkel
darkness	dunkelheit/finshtahnis
daughter	dochtah
daughter-in-law	shviah-dochtah
day	dawk
day after tomorrow	ivvah-meiya
day of preparation	risht-dawk
day of punishment	shtrohf-dawk
day of slaughter	shlacht-dawk
dead	doht
deaf	dawb
deal with	handla
death angel	dohdes-engel
debt	shuld
deceitful	shlitzoahrich
deceive	fafiahra
deceiver	fafiahrah
deception	fafiahrahrei

deceptiveness	fafiahrichkeit
decide	ausmacha
decree a ruling	eisetza
deep	deef
defect (n)	fayl
define	ausdrawwa
definition	auslayying
deliverance	frei-shtelling
deliverer	frei-drayyah
deny	falaykla
depart	falossa
desirable	ohgnaymd
desire (n)	falanga/falanging/glushta/lusht/villa
desire (v)	falanga/glushta/lushta
desire another's ill fortune	fagunna
desirous	glushtich
despise	fa'achta
destruction	fedeahving
devil	Deivel
devilish	deivilish
devour	fressa
diaper cloth	vindla-duch
die	shtauva/shteahva/umkumma
difference	unnahshitt
dig (v)	grawva
dig around	fagrawva
dig out	ausgrawva
diligence	fleisichkeit
diligent	fleisich
dill	dill
dilute	fadinnahra
dip (v)	dunka

directly	grawt
dirt	drekk
dirty	drekkich
disagreed (adj)	unaynich
disappear	fagay
disciple	yingah
discuss	fahandla/fashvetza
disgrace (n)	shand
disgraceful	shandlich
dishes	ksha
dishonest	uneahlich
disobedient	ungehorsam
disorder	unadning
dispense	ausdayla
distinct	deidlich
distinguishable	unnahshidlich
distribute	ausgevva
disunity	* unaynichkeit
ditch (n)	grawwa
division of priests	preeshtah-adning
do	du
doctor	doktah
doctrinally correct	saund
dog	hund
dollar	dawlah
dominance	ivvah-hand
don (v)	ohzeeya
donation	kshenkah-geld
donation box	geld-box
done (adj)	faddich
donkey	aysel
donkey colt	aysel-hutsh

door	deah
door of sheepfold	shohf-doah
door, large	doah
doorkeeper	deah-heedah
double-edged	zvay-shneidich
doubt (v)	zveifla
dough	dayk
dove	daub
down (separable prefix)	um
down from above	runnah
down here	hunna
down payment	nunnah-betzawling
down there	drunna
downward	nunnah
drag (v)	shlayfa
dragon	dracha-diah
dream (n)	drohm
dream (v)	drohma
dreamer	drohmah
dress (n)	rokk
dress (v)	ohdu
drink (animals) (v)	saufa
drink (n)	drink
drink (v)	drinka
drink an alcoholic beverage	saufa
drink in	eidrinka
drink offering	drink-opfah
drinking of alcoholic beverages	saufahrei
drive a vehicle	foahra
drive out	ausdreiva
drive, chase	dreiva
drop of blood	bloots-drobba

dropsy	vassah-sucht
drown	fasaufa
dry (adj)	drukka
dry (v)	drikla
dust	shtawb
dwell	voona
dwelling	vohning
dwelling place	voon-blatz

E

each	yaydah
each other	nannah
eagle	awdlah
ear	oah
earlier	foahheah
earlier time	foahzeit
early	free
earn	fadeena
earnestly	eahnshtlich
earnestness	eahnshtlichkeit
earth	eaht
earthen	eahdich
earthly	eahtlich
earthquake	eaht-bayben
east	eest
Easter	Ohshtah
easy	eesi
eat	essa
eaten away	fafressa
edge of a sword	shvadda-shnitt
education	lanning
egg	oi

eight	acht
eighteen	achtzay
eighty	achtzich
either, or	eedah/endveddah, adda
elder (church)	eldishtah
eleven	elf
eleventh	elft
embarrassed, to be	shemma
emotional feeling	kfeel
emotionally affected	bevaykt
emphasize with expletives	fagrefticha
empty	leah
enact	ausfiahra
encourage	ufmundahra
end (v)	enda
endure	aushalda
endure patiently	ohnemma
enemy	feind
energetic	rawsich
enough	genunk
ensure	seiya
enthusiasm	moot
entice	lokka
entire	gans
entrust	fadrauwa
envious	fagunnish/fagunshtlich/ohgunnish
envy (n)	fagunsht/ohgunsht
envy (v)	fagunna
equal (adj)	gleich/-a/-lich
error	faylah
escaped (adj)	haus
especially	patiklah

establish	grunda
establish in office	eisetza
esteem	ohdenka
esteem lightly	fa'achta
esteemed highly	hohch-gacht
eternal	ayvich
eternally	ayvichlich
eternity	ayvichkeit
ethnic group	kshlecht
eunuch	kemmahrah
evangelistic	effangaylish
Eve	Ayfaw
even, level	ayva
evening	ohvet
evening meal	ohvet-essa
evening red	ohvet-roht
ever	evvah, salayva
every	alli
everywhere	ivvahrawl
evil	eevil
exactly	grawt
examine a matter	unnah-sucha
example	foahbild
except	ausgnumma
excessively	ivvah-dimaws/zu
excuse (n)	ausret
excuse (v)	ausredda
executor	eahbshaft-daylah
exorcise	beshveahra
exorcist	beshveahrah
expensive	deiyah
expire	ausgevva

expositor	auslayyah
extinguish	ausmacha
extinguished, to become	ausgay
extra	extri
extremely	heslich
eye (n)	awk
eye salve	awwa-shmiah

F

fable	fawbel
face (n)	ksicht
fail (v)	fayla
faithful	voahhaftich
fall (v)	falla
fall asleep	eishlohfa
false	falsh
false appearance	fashtelling
falsehood	falshhayt/-heit
familiar	bekand
family	shtamm
famine	hungahs-noht
fancy	fei
far	veit
fare (v)	ausmacha
farm (n)	bavvahrei
farmer	bavvah
fast (adj) (adv)	shteik
fast (v)	fashta
fast day	fasht-dawk
fast talk, persuade	fashvetza
fastened (adj)	fesht
fat	fett

109

father (n)	daett
father of a household	haus-faddah
fault (n)	shuld
fault finder	faylah-suchah
fawn upon	shmaychla
fear (n)	furcht
fear (v)	feicha
fear of God	Gottes-furcht
fearful	feichbutzich
fearless	feichtlohs
feast	fesht
feast of bread	broht-fesht
feast of dedication	tempel-fesht
feather	feddah
feed (v)	feedahra
feel (v)	feela
fellow	kall
fellow elder	mitt-eldishtah
fellow heir	mitt-eahvah
fellow servant	mitgnecht/mitt-deenah
fellow soldier	mitt-shtreidah
fellowship	gmeinshaft
female person	veibsmensh
fence (n)	fens
fetch	hohla
fetter (n)	band
few	vennich
field (n)	feld
field of blood	bloot-feld
field with crop in it	frucht-feld
fiery	feiyahrich
fifteen	fuftzay

fifty	fuftzich
fig tree	feiya-bohm
fight (n)	fecht
fight (v)	fechta
fighter	fechtah
fighting	gefecht
fighting against	viddah-shtreit
figs	feiya
fill (v)	filla
finally	endlich
find (v)	finna
find out	ausfinna
finger (n)	fingah
fire (n)	feiyah
fire oven	feiyah-offa
first	seahsht
firstborn	eahsht-geboahra
firstfruit	eahsht-frucht
first one	eahsht
fish (v)	fisha
fish line	fish-lein
fisher	fishah
fist	fausht
five	fimf
flame (n)	flamm
flame of fire	feiyah-flamm
flash (v)	blitza
flee	fleeya
flesh	flaysh
fleshly	flayshlich
fleshly desire	vohlusht
flood (n)	flott

floor (n)	bodda/floah
flower (n)	blumm
flute	peif
flute-player	peifah/peif-shpeelah
fly (v)	fleeya
foam (n)	shaum
fog	nevvel
foliage	lawb
follies	dumhayda
follow	folya/nohch-folya/nohch-macha
follower	nohch-folyah/nohch-machah
following	nohch
food	ess-sach/shpeis
fool (n)	nah
foolish	naddish
foolishness	dumhaydichkeit
foot	foos
footer	fuddah
footsteps	foos-dabba
footstool	foos-shtool
for	fa
forbid	fabeeda
force (n)	foahs
forefather	foahfaddah
forefathers	foaheldra
forehead	shtann
foreign to Greece	Ungreeyish
foreigner	auslendah
foresight	foahdenkes/foahsicht
forest fire	bush-feiyah
forever	fa'immah
forget	fagessa

forgive	fagevva
formerly	eahshtah
forswear	fashveahra
forth	foah
fortune teller	voah-sawwah
forty	fatzich
forward	faddi/fassich
forward most	feddahsht
fountain	brunna
four	fiah
four-footed	fiah-feesich
four-cornered	fiah-ekkich
fourteen	fatzay
fourteenth	fatzayt
fox	fox
free (adj)	frei
freedom	freiheit
fresh	frish
friend	freind
friendliness	freindlichkeit
friendly	freindlich
fringe	fransel
frog	frosh
from	difunn/funn
from above	ovva-heah
front, at the	fanna
fruit	frucht/obsht
fruitful	fruchtboah
fulfill	folfilla
full	foll
fully	folshtendich/-lich
fulness	folheit

funds for charity	oahma-geld
funeral	leicht
funeral song	leicht-leet
funny	dumm/fannich
furious	zannich
fuss (n)	vaysa

G

gallon	gall
garden	goahra
gardener	goahra-haldah
garment	glayt
garment bag	glaydah-sakk
garment of sackcloth	sakk-glayt
gate	doah
gather	geddahra/samla
gather in	eisamla
gathering (n)	samling
gaunt	mawwa
gear wheel	kumrawt
genealogy	freindshaft-regishtah/freindshaft-shtamm
generation	kshlecht
generous	mitt-daylich
Gentile	Heid
genuine	voahhaftich
get	greeya
ghost	kshpukk
gift	kshenk
girl	maydel
give	gevva
give without charge	shenka

giver	gevvah
giving of thanks	dankes
glad	froh
gladly	geahn
glass (material)	glaws
glass, made of	glawsich
glass (water)	glaws
glassy	glawsich
glittering	glitzahrich
glorify	fakleahra
glorious	hallich
glory	gloahheit/hallichkeit
glutton (n)	fressah
glutton (v)	fressa
gluttony	fressahrei
gnat	mikli
go	gay
goat	gays
goatskin	gaysa-haut
God fearing	Gottes-firchtich
goddess	gettin
Godhead	Gottheit
godless	gottlohs
godliness	getlichkeit
godly	getlich
golden	goldich
good	goot
goodness	geedichkeit
good-smelling	goot-shmakkich
goose	gans
government	ovvahrichkeit
grab (v)	graebba

grace (n)	gnawdi/gnawt
graft (v)	zveicha
grandchild	kins-kind
grandmother	grohs-mammi
grape	draub
grapevine	drauva-shtokk/vei-shtokk
grasshopper	hoi-shrekk
grave (n)	begraybnis/fagrawbnis/grawb
greedy	greedich
Greek	greeyish
green	gree
greet	greesa
greeting	groos
grieved	bedreebt
grind (v)	mawla
grinding wheel	meel-shtay
ground (n)	bodda
ground, establish	grunda
group	drubb
group of applicants for drawing lots	lohs
grow	vaxa
grumble	grumla
grumbler	grumlah
gully	grawva

H

habit	gebrauch
had	katt
hail	shlohsa
hailstones	shlohsa
hair	hoah
half	halb/helft

hand	hand
handkerchief	shnubb-duch
handle (v)	haendla
handwriting	hand-shreives
hang	henka
hang onto	ohhenka
happen	gevva
happening	kshicht
hard	hatt
hard of hearing	hatt-heahrich
hardworking	hatt-shaffich
harden	fahadda
harm (v)	shadda
harness (n)	ksha
harp	harf
harp player	harf-shpeelah
harvest (n)	eahn/-d
harvest (v)	eisamla
hate (v)	hassa
hated (adj)	fahast
hateful	fahast
haul (v)	foahra
have	havva
have in excess	shpeahra
hay	hoi
he	ah/eah
head (n)	kobb
headfirst	kobb-feddahsht
heal	hayla
heal by magic	braucha
health	ksundhayt
healthy	ksund

hear	heahra
hearing ability	heahrich
hearing, to give a	faheahra
heart	hatz
heartfelt	hatzlich
heartily	greftichlich
hearty	greftich
heat (n)	hitz
heaven	Himmel
heavenly	himlish
heavenly establishment	Himmelshaft
heavy	shveah
heavyset	ksetzt
heed	achta
heifer	rind
height	haych
heir	eahvah
hell	hell
hell fire	hell-feiyah
hellish	hellish
helmet	greeks-hoot
help (v)	helfa
helper	helfah/mitt-helfah
hen (setting)	glukk
her	es/iahra/see
herb plant	rauda-shtokk
herbs	greidah
here	do
hers	iahra/sei
hide (v)	fashtekla
high	hohch
highest	alli-haychsht

Highest	Alli-Haychsht
hill	hivvel
him	eem/een/en
hinder	fahinnahra
hindrance	hinnahnis
hip	hift
hire	dinga
hire out	fadinga
his	sei
hit (v)	shlauwa
hit or make contact	dreffa
hoe (n)	hakk
hoe (v)	hakka
hold (v)	hayva
hold out, endure	aushayva
hole	loch
hole in the earth	grund-loch
holiday	feiyah-dawk
holiest	alli-heilichsht
holy	heilich
Holy Spirit	Heilig Geisht
home (adv)	haym
home (n)	haymet
honest	eahlich/ufrichtich
honesty	ufrichtichkeit
honor (n)	eah
honor (v)	eahra
honored (adj)	ohgnaymd
hope (n)	hofning
hope (v)	hoffa
horn	hann/blohs-hann (music)
horse	gaul

horse in hitch	fuah
horse team	fuah
horseman	geils-mann
hot	hays
hotel	shlohf-haus
hour	shtund
house	haus
household	haus-hohld/-halding
how	vi
human (adj)	menshlich
human (n)	mensh
humble (adj)	daymeedich
humble (v)	daymeedicha
humility	daymoot
hunger (n)	hungah
hungry	hungahrich
hurry (v)	dumla
hurt (verb, intransitive)	shmatza
husband	mann
husk (n)	basht
hustle	rawsa
hypocrite	heichlah

I

I	ich
I belong	heahrich
I give	gevvich
I have	havvich
I hear	heahrich
I say	sawwich
I was	voahrich
idol	abgott

idol, likeness of	abgott- gleichness
idolatrous	abgeddish
idolatry	abgeddahrei
if (conjunction)	vann
ignite (verb, intransitive)	ohgay
illuminated by daylight	dawk
image	bild
imitate	nohch-macha
immediately	grawt
immoderate	unksheit
immorality	lushtahrei
imperishable	unfagenglich
impossible	unmeeklich
improper (adj)	unkshikt
improper (adv)	unshiklich
improve	fabessahra
impure	unrein
impurity	unreinichkeit
in	in
in a	imma/innen
in addition	shunsht
in from outside	rei
in front of	fannich
in return or reply (adv)	zrikk
in that case	dann
in the	im
in the daytime	dawks
in there	drinn
incarcerate	eishtekka
incense altar	insens-awldah
incense cup	insens-kobli
incite	hetza

121

include	einemma
included (adj)	dibei
incomprehensible	unbegreiflich
increase (v)	fameahra
incur	ohbringa
indebted to	shuldich
indeed	even
indifferent	aldvannish
inexpressible	unshprechlich
infect	ohshtekka
inherit	eahva
inheritance	eahbshaft
inheritance of children	kinnah-eahbshaft
ink	dinda
innocent	unshuldich
insert (v)	shtekka
inside	inseid
inside, on the	invendich
insight	eiseit/eisicht
instantly	bletzlich
insult (n)	hakk
intemperance	unfashtendlichkeit
intemperate	unfashtendlich/unksheit
interest (financial)	indressa
interjection	ei
internally	innahlich
interrogate	ausfrohwa
intestines	deahm
intoxicated	ksoffa
invite	haysa
invoice	bill
inward (direction)	nei

iron	eisa
iron, made of	eisich
is	is
it	es
its	sei

J

jail (n)	kfengnis
jar (n)	tsheah
Jew	Yutt
Jewish	Yiddish
Jewish church	Yudda-gmay
Jewish Council	Yudda-council
joints of bones	gveahva
joy	frayt/freyyaheit
joyful	fraylich
joyfulness	fraylichkeit
judge (n)	richtah
judge (v)	richta
judgment	gericht/gerichtichkeit/richtichkeit
judgment day	gerichts-dawk/richtah-dawk
judgment hall	richt-haus
judgment place	richts-blatz
judgment seat	richtah-shtool
jump (v)	tshumba

K

keep	halda
keep in remembrance	eidenka
kernel	kann
kettle	kessel
key	shlissel

kill (v)	umbringa
kind	goot-maynich
kind of, sort	satt
kindness	goot-maynichkeit
king	kaynich
kingdom	reich
kingdom of heaven	Himmel-reich
kiss (n)	kuss
kiss (v)	kissa
knee (n)	gnee
knock on a door (v)	globba/ohglobba
know (information or facts)	vissa
know ahead of time	foahvissa
knowledge	vissaheit

L

lacking understanding	unfashtendlich
lamb	lamm
lame	lohm
lamentable	yammahlich
land	land
landscape	landshaft
language	shprohch
lantern	ladann
lap	shohs
lash (v)	fagayshla
last	letsht
late	shpoht
later	shpaydah
laugh (v)	lacha
laundry	vesh
law (Old Testament)	ksetz

law giver	ksetz- gevvah
lawbreaker	ksetz-brechah
lawless	unadlich
lawn	hohf
lay	layya
lay off	ablayya
lay on, apply	ohlayya
lazy	faul
lead (v)	fiahra/foahgay
leader	foahgayyah/foahgengah
leaf (n)	blatt
learn	lanna
leather	leddah
leave behind	lossa
leave on, to not extinguish	ohlossa
leave on, to not remove	ohlossa
left (direction)	lings
left over	ivvahrich
leg	bay
lend	layna/shpeahra
length	leng
length of a street	shtrohsa-leng
lengthen	falengahra
leprosy	aussatz
leprous	aussetzich
letter of alphabet	bushtawb
letter of divorce	divorce-shreives
letter of praise	lohb-breef
letter, written communication	breef
level (adj)	ayva
lever	leevah
liar	leeyah/leeknah

licentiousness	unzucht
lie (n)	leek
lie, assume prone position	leiya
lie, tell an untruth	leeya
life	layva
life long	layves-lang
lifetime	layves-zeit
light (n)	licht
light a fire or lamp	ohmacha/ohshtekka
light colored	hell/leicht
lighthearted	leicht-hatzich
light up	uflichta
light weight	leicht
light, property of	helling
lightning	gviddah/veddah-laych
lightning, to flash	veddah-laycha
lightstand	licht-shtaend
like (v)	gleicha
like, as	vi
liken to	fagleicha
likeness	fagleichnis/gleichnis
likewise	gleichaveis
linen fabric	linnen duch
lion	layb
lip	left
listen	abheicha/heicha/ohheicha
little bit	bisli/bissel
live (v)	layva
livelihood	fadeensht
livestock	fee
load (v)	lawda
load down	nunnah-lawda

loaf (n)	layb
lock in	eishleesa
lock up	fashleesa
long (adj)	lang
look (v)	gukka
look ahead	foahgukka
look at	ohgukka
look out	ausgooka
loose	lohs
Lord	Hah
lose	faliahra
loud	laut
lovable	leeblich
love (v)	leeva
love feast	leebensmawl
low	niddah
lukewarm	lebbish
lump	glumba
lust (n)	falusht/lusht
lust (v)	lushta
lustful	lushtboah
lustfulness	lushtboahkeit

M

magistrate	shtatt-richtah
maid servant	deensht-mawt
maid, hired	mawt
majesty	kaynich-eah
make	macha
make over	ivvah-macha
male person	manskal
malice	fagunsht

man	mann/manskal
manger	foodah-drohk
manure	misht
many	en haufa/feel/en latt/en mannich
mark (n)	meik
mark (v)	meika
mark upon	fameika
market building	kawf-haus
marry	heiyahra
marvel (n)	vundah/vunnah
master (n)	meishtah
matter (v)	ausmacha/shadda
matter, affair	sach
may, be allowed	mawk
maybe	fleicht
me	mich/miah (dative case)
meal	eems/essa
mean (v)	mayna
meaning (n)	mayning
measure (n)	maws
measure (v)	messa
measure out	ausmessa
meat market	flaysh-market
meek	sanftmeedich
meekness	sanftmeedichkeit/sanftmoot
meet (v)	ohdreffa
melt	fashmelsa
member	gleet
memorized	ausvennich
men folk	mansleit
mend	flikka
merchant	kayfah

merchants	kawf-leit
merciful	bamhatzich
merciful, to be	aboahma
merciless	unbamhatzich
mercy	bamhatzichkeit
mercy seat	gnawda-shtool
midnight	halb-nacht/mitt-nacht
might (v)	mechta
mile	meil
milk (n)	millich
mill	meel
mind (n)	meind
minded (adj)	psunna
mint plant	mint-blansa
miracle worker	zaycha-shaffah
miraculous sign	zaycha
mirror (n)	shpikkel
miss, fail to meet	fafayla
mock (v)	falacha/fashpodda/shpodda
mocker	shpoddah
moderation	fashtand
money	geld
money bag	geld-sakk
money changer	geld-vexlah
money lenders	layns-leit
month	moonet
mood	moot
more	may
morning	meiya
morning red	meiya-roht
morning star	meiya-shtann
mortal (adj)	shteahblich

most	mensht
moth	shawb
mother	maemm
mother-in-law	shviah-muddah
Mount of Olives	ayl-berg
mountain	berg
mouth	maul
move (v)	farayya
move to another residence	zeeya
mow (v)	mayya
much	feel
mulberry	maulbeahra
murderer	doht-shlayyah/maddah
murderous actions	maddahrei
must	missa
mustard	moshtaht
my	mei/meim

N

nail (v)	nakla
nail hole	nakkel-loch
naked	blutt/nakkich
name (n)	nohma
name (v)	haysa/nohma
name of blasphemy	leshtah-nohma
named, to be	haysa
namely	naymlich
narrate	fazayla
narrow	eng/shmawl
nation, people	folk
natives	lands-leit
natural	nadiahlich

natured	naduaht
near	nayksht
nearly	ball/baut/shiah
necessary	nohdvendich
necessity	noht
neck	hals
need (v)	braucha
needle (n)	nohdel
neighbor	nochbah
neighborhood	nochbahshaft
nest	nesht
net	nett
never	nee/neemols
new	nei/neiya
news	zeiya
next	neksht
nice	shay
night	nacht
nine	nein
ninety	neintzich
ninety-nine	neina-neintzich
ninth	neind
no	nay
no longer	nimmi
no one	nimmand
noble birth, of	hohch-geboahra
noise	yacht
noisy	yachtich
none	kenn/kens
nonresistant	veahlohs
noon	middawk
noon meal	middawk

north	natt
northwest	natt-vest
not	naett/nett
not any	kenn
nothing	nix
notice (v)	fameika
nourishment	layves-mawl
now	nau
nowadays	heidich's dawk
nowhere	neiyetz

O

oath	fashteiking
obey	heicha
obligation	shuldichkeit
occupation	eahvet
occur	ohgay
of	funn
of a	fu'ma/funn'ra
of course	voll
of the	fu'm
off	ab
off (pref)	ab
offense	eiyahniss
offense, to take	shtohsa
offensive (adj)	eiyahlich
offer (v)	beeda/ohbeeda
offering (to idols)	getza-opfah
offering for sin	sind-opfah
offering of praise	lohb-opfah
office (apostolic)	aposhtel-deensht
officer	ivvah-deenah

often	oft
oftentimes	als
oil	ayl
oil used for anointing	salba-ayl
ointment	greidah-ayl
old	ald
olive berry	ayl-frucht
olive tree	ayl-bohm
on there	druff
on, upon	uf
one (number)	ay/aym/ayn/aynra/ayns
one (pronoun)	ma (nominative case)
one of several	aynd/end
one tenth	zeyyadel
one time	mohl
one's own	aykna/ayya
one's self	em
only one	aynsisht
only yet	eahsht
only, just	yusht
onward, along	zvayk
open	uf
open area	uffana
opinion	mayning
opinion, to have an	mayna
opportunity	gleyyaheit
opposed, against	geyyich/viddah
opposed, to be	digeyya
opposition	viddah-shtand
opposition, verbal	viddahbat
or	adda
ordain	eisetza

order	addah
orderliness	adning
other	annah
otherwise, else	annahshtah/shunsht
out here	haus
out of	aus, raus
out there	draus
outer ones	ausahri
outermost	ausahsht
outside	ausah/autseid
outside, on the	ausahlich/ausvendich
outsider	autseidah
outward (direction)	naus
oven	offa
over	ivvah
over (direction)	nivvah
over there	drivva
overcome	ivvah-kumma
overcomer	ivvah-kummah
overeat	fressa
overflow (v)	ivvah-lawfa
overlay (v)	ivvah-layya
overlook (v)	ivvah-gukka
overnight	ivvah-nacht
oversee	ivvah-sayna
overseer	ivvah-saynah
overtake	ivvah-nemma
overthrow	umshmeisa
owe	aykna
own (v)	aykna
ox	ox

P

pail	aymah
pain (n)	shmatz
painful	vay
pale	blayyich
palm tree	palma
paper	babiah
parable	fagleichnis/gleichnis
pardon (v)	shenka
parents	eldra
particle	flekka
particular	patiklah
Passover feast	Ohshtah-fesht
Passover lamb	Ohshtah-lamm
past	fabei/ivvah
pasture	vayt
path	pawt
patience	geduld/-heit
patient	geduldich
pattern (n)	mushtah
pay (v)	bezawla
payer of debts	zrikk-bezawlah
payment	bezawling
peace	fridda
peacefully	fridlich
people	leit
perceive	fanemma
perfect (adj)	folkumma
perfection	folkummaheit
perform	ausfiahra
permission	alawbniss

persecute	fafolka/-ya
persevere	shtikka
persuade	ivvah-vinna
persuaded	gvunna
phylactery	bayt-box
piece (n)	shtikk
pierce	shtecha
piercing (noise)	hell
pig	sau
pile (n)	haufa
pile together	heifla
pillow (n)	kissi
pilot (n)	shtiah-mann
pious	fromm
pipe for smoking	peif
pitiful	eahmlich
pitiful condition	oahmoot
pity (v)	davvahra
place (n)	blatz
plague (n)	blohk
plan ahead	foahzayla
plan on	fikkahra
plank	blank
plant (n)	blansa/shtokk
plant (v)	blansa
plant, small	shtekli
plate (n)	dellah
play (v)	shpeela
please (v)	sooda
pleasure	blesiah/vohl-kfalla
pleat (n)	fald
plow (n)	blook

plow (v)	bloowa
point (n)	shpitza
point, conclusion	punka
pointed tool for piercing	shtechah
pointer on an instrument	zaycha
poison (n)	gift
poison (v)	fagifta
poisonous	giftich
poke (v)	renna
poor (adj)	oahm
porch	poatsh
portion (n)	dayl/shiah
portion received by lot	lohs
possible	meeklich
pound (n)	pund
pour	leahra
pour out	ausleahra
poverty	oahmoot
power (n)	gvald/macht
powerful	gvaldich
powers of heaven	Himmels-grefta
praise (n)	lohb
praise (v)	lohva/preisa
praised highly	hohch-gelohbt
pray	bayda
prayer house	bayt-haus
preach	breddicha
preacher	breddichah/leahrah
preaching	breddiches/gebreddich
precious	keshtlich
precisely	pinklich
predetermine	foahrichta

137

predict	foahsawwa
predict, tell a fortune	voah-sawwa
preeminence	foahgang
preeminent	foahnaymsht
prefix meaning at, about, of	droh
prefix meaning in	ei
prepare	rishta
prepare ahead of time	foahrishta
presently	allaveil
press (v)	drikka
pretend	ohlossa
prettiness	shayheit
prevent	fahalda
pride	hohchmoot
priesthood	preeshtahshaft/-tum
prince	kaynichs-sohn
print (v)	drukka
privilege	gleyyaheit
probably	andem
proclaim	fakindicha
progressive tense indicator	am
promise (n)	fashpreching/fashprechnis
promise (v)	fashprecha
prophecy	brofayda-vadda/broffetzeiying
prophesy	broffetzeiya
prophet	brofayt
prophetess	brofayda-veib
prophetic words	broffetzeiya-vadda
prostitute	huah
prostitution	huahrahrei
proud	hohchmeedich/shtols
proverb	shprich-vatt

publish (for marriage)	ausroofa
puddle	drekk-loch
pull (v)	zeeya
pull apart into pieces	farobba
punish	shtrohfa
punishment	shtrohf
pure	rein
purification	reiniching
purify	reinicha
purity	reinichkeit
purposely	poahbes
push (v)	sheeva
put	du
put on, wear	ohdu

Q

quarter	faddel
question (n)	frohk
quick	dabbah/kshvind/shnell
quiet	ruich

R

rate, form an opinion of	ohsayna
rather	leevah
rave	rawsa
raving	rawsich
reach (v)	langa
read	laysa
reader	laysah
reap	eahnda
reasonable	fashtendich/-lich/ksheit
reasonableness	fashtendlichkeit

recently	katzlich
recognize	kenna
recompense (n)	lohn
region	landshaft
regret (v)	shpeida
rein in	eirayna
reject	zrikk-stohsa
rejoice	froiya
related by blood or marriage	difreind
relatives	freindshaft
relinquish control of	ivvah-gevva/ivvah-lossa
reluctance	lasht
reluctance, to show	veahra
reluctant	falayt
remaining (adj)	ivvahrich
remember	meinda
remind	gmohna/ohgmohna
remove	abnemma
remove (clothing)	ausnemma
remove (entrails)	ausnemma
renewed	nei-gmacht
repent	bekeahra
repentance	boos
repulsive	grausam/-lich
request	bidda
resist	shteibahra
rest (n)	roo
rest (v)	roowa
restless	unruich
restrain	eirayna
resurrection	uffashtaying
revelation	offenboahring/veising

revenge, to take	auseeva/ausnemma
revengeful	auseevish
revenger	zrikk-betzawlah
revolting	grausam/-lich
rhubarb	shtengel
rich	reich
riches	reichtum
richly	reichlich
richness	reichheit/reichlichkeit
ride (v)	foahra/reida
ride	reidah
right, correct	recht
right, toward the	rechts
righteous	gerecht
righteousness	gerechtichkeit
ring (n)	band
risky	unksheit
road	vayk
rob	rawva
robber	rawvah
robe	mandel
rod, staff	root
roll (v)	rolla
roof of a house	haus-dach
room (n)	kammah/shtubb
rooster	hohna
root (n)	vatzel
rope (n)	shtrikk
rot	fafaula
rotten	faul
round about	rumm-heah
rub	reiva

rub out	ausreiva
rudder	shtiah-boaht
rumor	kshvetz
run	shpringa
run down, slander	nunnah-ranna
rust (n)	rosht
rust (v)	faroshta

S

sack	sakk
sackcloth	sakk-duch
sacrifice (n)	opfah
sacrifice (v)	opfahra
sacrificial lamb	opfah-lamm
safe	sayf
sailor	shiff-gnecht
sake	sayk
salt	sals
salty	salsich
salvation	saylichkeit
salve (n)	shmiah
same	gleich/-a/-lich/saym
sanctify	heilicha
sand (n)	sand
Satan	Satan
satiated	satt
saved	saylich
Saviour	Heiland
saw (n)	sayk
saw (v)	sayya
scales for measuring weight	vohk
scales, to remove	shawva

scare (v)	fashrekka
scatter	fashtroiya/shtroiya
scent	kshmakk
schism	shpalding
school	shool
schoolmaster	shool-meishtah
scold	fagrumla/fashelda/zanka
scoop (v)	shebba
scourge (n)	gayshel
scourge (v)	gayshla
scourging (n)	gayshtling
scrape away	shadda
scrape off	shawva
scratch over the surface	shadda
scream (v)	greisha
scribe	shrift-geleahrah
Scriptural	effangaylish
Scriptures	Shrift
sea	say
seal (n)	seel
seam (n)	noht/sohm
search out	ausgooka
seat (n)	sitz
second one	zvett
see	sayna
seed	sohma
seek	sucha
seem	dinka/gmohna
self	selvaht/sich
selfish desire for glory	eahgeitz
sell	fakawfa
send	shikka

separate (v)	fadayla
separate by passing through a sieve	seena
separated	funn-nannah
servant	deenah/deensht-gnecht/gnecht
servanthood	gnechtshaft
servants	deensht-leit
serve	abvoahra
service to God	Gottes-deensht
set an example	foahbilda
set forth	foahshtella
set in authority	ivvah-setza
set in leadership	foahsetza
set or place (v)	shtella
settle	sedla
settle a matter	ausrichta
seven	sivva
seventh	sivvet
seventh one	sivveda
seventy	sivvetzich
several	edlichi/poah
sew	nayya
shake (v)	shidla
shake off	abshidla
shake out	ausshidla
shall	soll/mawk
shame (n)	shohm
shame (v)	fashohma
share (v)	mitt-dayla
sharer of similar fate	mitt-daylah
sharp	shauf
shave (v)	shayfa
shawl	shawl

she	es/see
sheep	shohf
sheepfold	shohf-shtall
sheepskin	shohf-haut
shelf (n)	lawda
shepherd	shohf-heedah
shine (v)	sheina
ship (n)	shiff
shipmaster	shiff-meishtah
shirt	hemm
shiver (v)	ziddahra
shoe	shoo
shoestring	shoo-bandel
short	katz
shortcut, by	grawtzu
shorten	fakatza
should	sedda/sella/soll
shoulder (n)	shuldah
shout (n)	grish
shove (v)	renna
shovel (n)	shaufel
show (v)	veisa
showbread	tempel-broht
shrink (v)	eigay
sick	grank/shlecht
sickle	sichel
sickly	eahmlich
sickness	granket/-heit
side	seit
side up with	eiseida
sidestep	ausdredda
sift	sifta

silken	seida
silver	silvah
silversmith	silvah-shmitt
similar fate	mitt-dayl
similar portion	mitt-dayl
sin (n)	sind
sin (v)	sindicha
sin flood	sindfloot
since	siddah
sinews	flexa
sinful	sindfol/-lich
sing	singa
singe	fasenka
singer	singah
sinner	sindah
sister	shveshtah
sit	hokka
six	sex
sixteen	sechtzay
sixth	sext
sixty	sechtzich
skull	shkoll
skull place	shkoll-blatz
slaughter (n)	shlacht
slaughter (v)	shlachta/shlawdra
sleep (n)	shlohf
sleep (v)	shlohfa
sleeper	shlayfah
sleepy	shlayfahrich
slow	shloh
sluggard	faulensah
small	glay

small amount	vennich
small distance	shtikk
small lump of dough	daykli
small, fine	fei
smart	shmeaht
smear (v)	fashmiahra
smell (v)	shmakka
smelly	shmakkich
smith	shmitt
smoke (n)	shmohk
smoke (v)	shmohka
smooth (adj)	glatt
smother	fashtikka
snake (n)	shlang
snare (n)	fang-shtrikk
snow (n)	shnay
so	so
soap	sayf
sober	sohbah
socially inept	ungland
softhearted	vayyich-hatzich
soil (v)	fadrekka
soldier	greeks-deenah/-gnecht/-mann
some	dayl/samm
someone	ebbah
something	ebbes
sometimes	alsamohl
somewhere	eiyetz
son	sohn
song	leet
song of praise	lohb-leet
soon	ball/glei

sorcerer	hexah/zahbahrah
sorcery	hexahrei
sore (adj)	vay
sort of, rather	sadda
sound to someone	lauda
sound, healthy	saund
sound, noise	saund
sound, to make a rushing	rausha
sour (adj)	savvah
sour (v)	fasavvahra
sourdough, leaven	savvah-dayk
south	sauda
South	sayt
Southwest	saut-vest
souvenir	ohdenkes
sow (n)	lohs/sau
sow (v)	sayya
sower	sayyah
space (n)	blatz
spare, save from	shpeahra
sparrow	shpatz
speak argumentatively	eiyahra
spear (n)	shpees/shpiah
spear (v)	shpeesa
speech, manner of	kshvetz
spend	shpenda
spill (v)	fageesa
spirit	geisht
spirit of servitude	gnechta-geisht
spiritual	geishtlich
spirituality	geishtlichkeit
spit (v)	shpautza

spittle	shpautz
splinter	shliffah
split (v)	fashpalda
spoil	fadauva/fadeahva
spot (n)	blakka/flekka
spread apart (adv)	ausnannah
spread bedding for livestock	shtroiya
spring of water	vassah-shpring
sprinkle (v)	shpritza
sprinkle with a liquid (v)	ohshpritza
squander (v)	fablohsa
squeeze (v)	drikka/fadrikka
squirm	gveahva
stain spot	flekka
stairs	shtayk
stall (n)	shtall
stamp (v)	shtamba
stand (n)	shtaend
stand (v)	shtay
standards, church	adning
star (n)	shtann
start (v)	shteahra
start off	abshteahra
starve	fahungahra
stay (v)	bleiva
steadfast	shtandhaftich
steadfastness	shtandhaftichkeit
steal (v)	shtayla
stealing, habitual	geshtayl
stem	shtamm/shtengel
stepmother	shteef-maemm
steward	haus-haldah

stewardship	haus-haldes/haus-halding
stick (n)	shtekka
stick to	shtekka
stick, small	shtekli
stiff	shteif
still, quiet	shtill
still, yet	alsnoch
sting (v)	shtecha
stinger	shtechah
stink (v)	shtinka
stir (v)	riahra/shtadda/shtarra
stomach	bauch/mawwa
stone (n)	shtay
stone (v)	shtaynicha
stone tablet	shtay-tablet
stony	shtaynich
stoop (v)	bikka
stop (v)	shtobba
store (n)	shtoah
storehouse	shtoah-haus
storm	shtoahm
stormy	stoahmich
story	kshicht/shtoahri
straight	grawt
strange	ab/fremd/kshpassich
streak (n)	shtraych
street	shtrohs
strength	graft/grefta
strengthen	fagrefticha/fashteika
strict	shtreng
strife	zank
string (n)	bendel

stroke (n)	shtraych
stroke, small	shtrichli
strong	greftich/shteik
strongly	greftichlich
stubborn	dikk-kebbich/fashtokt/shteibahrich
stumble	shtatza/shtolbahra
stumbling block	shtolbah-blakk
stumblingstone	shtolbah-shtay
suchlike	soddich/sohwich
suffer	leida/soffahra
suffocate	fashtikka
suit (v)	sooda
sulphur	shvevvel
summer	summah
sun (n)	sunn
sundown	sunn-unnah
supper	sobbah
supreme power	ivvah-macht
supremely powerful	ivvah-mechtich
sure, certain	geviss/shuah
surprise (v)	fagelshtahra
surrender (v)	eigevva
swallow (v)	shlukka
swear	shveahra
swear at	faflucha
sweat (n)	shvitz
sweep (v)	keahra
sweep out	auskeahra
swell (v)	kshvilla
swim (v)	shvimma
swineherd	sei-heedah
sword	shvatt
sympathize	mitt-leida

T

tabernacle	tent-tempel
table	dish
tail (n)	shvans
take (v)	nemma
take care of	seiya
take in	einemma
take over	ivvah-nemma
talk (v)	shvetza
talker	shvetzah
tame (adj)	zohm
tame (v)	zohma
tan (v)	taena
tanner	taenah
taste (v)	fasucha
tax collector	tax-einemmah
tax table	tax-dish
teach	leahra
teacher	leahrah/teetshah
teaching (n)	lanning
tear (v)	fareisa/reisa
tear out	ausreisa
tears	awwa-vassah
tease (v)	zarra
tell	fazayla
temperament	naduah
temperance	maws
temple	tempel
tempt	fasucha
tempter	fasuchah
ten	zeyya
tenth	zeyyet

terminate	ausgay
terrible	shlimm
terrifying	shreklich
test (v)	ausbroviahra
Testament	Teshtament
testament of property distribution	villa
tether (v)	ohbinna
thank	danka
thankful	dankboah
thankfulness	dankboahkeit
thanks	dank
that (demonstrative)	sell
that (relative pronoun)	es
the	da/di/es
the deep	deefa
their	iahra
theirs	iahra
them	eena/na (contraction)/si
then	no
there (adv)	datt
thereby	dideich
therefore	dann/drumm/so
they	si
thick	dikk
thief	deeb/shtaylah
thievery	shtaylahrei
thin out	fadinnahra
thing	ding/sach
think	denka
think over	ivvah-denka
third one	dridda/dritt
third part	driddel

153

thirst	dasht
thirsty	dashtich
thirty	dreisich
this	deah/deahra/dee/demm/dess
thistle	dishtel
thoroughly	ivvahraus
those	denna
thoughts	gedanka
thousand	dausend
threaten	droiya
three	drei
thresh	dresha
threshing floor	dresha-floah
throat	hals
throne	kaynich-shtool
through	deich
through it	dideich
throw (v)	shmeisa/shtohsa
thrust (n)	shtohs
thrust (v)	shtohsa
thunder (v)	dimla
thunderstorm	gviddah-shtoahm
tidy (adj)	zvayk
tidy up	ufrohma
tie (v)	binna
tie fast to	ohbinna
time (n)	zeit
time of punishment	shtrohf-zeit
tinkling	klinglich
tired	meet
tired of	laydich
to	zu/ditzu

today	heit
toe (n)	zeyya
together	zammah
tomorrow	meiya
tongue	zung
tonight	dinohvet
too (used to contradict)	avvah
torch	feiyah-shtekka
torment (v)	gvayla
touch (v)	ohrayya
toward	geyyich/ingeyya
toward former place or state	zrikk
toward here	heah/rivvah
toward there	hee
towel	hand-lumba
tower (n)	tavvah
town	shteddel/shtedli
trade (n)	vexel
trade (v)	fahandla/handla
trample	fadredda
transgress against	fashuldicha
translate	ivvah-setza
tread (v)	dredda
tread out	ausdredda
treasury	tempel-box
tree (n)	bohm
tremble	ziddahra
trespass (n)	ivvah-dredding
trespass (v)	ivvah-dredda
trespasser	ivvah-dreddah
trouble (n)	druvvel
trouble (v)	druvla

troublemaker	druvvel-machah
true	voah/voahhaftich
truly	veiklich/voahlich
trunk of a tree	shtamm
trust (v)	drauwa
truth	voahheit/voahret
try (v)	broviahra/fasucha
try out	ausbroviahra
tumult	ufruah
tune (n)	veis
turn (v)	drayya
turn on a light	ohmacha
turn out	ausdrayya
turn over	ivvah-drayya
turn, bend (n)	dray
turtle dove	daddel-daub
twelfth	zvelft
twelve	zvelf
twenty	zvansich
twig	fitz, hekk
twin	zvilling
two	zvay
two-faced	zvay-ksichtich

U

unaccomplished	unfaseikt
unbelief	unglawva
unbelieving	unglawvich
unborn	ungeboahra
uncared for	unfaseikt
uncircumcised	unbeshnidda
uncircumcision	unbeshneiding

unclean	unsauvah
unclothed	ungeglayt
unconcerned	unbekimmaht
unconscious	ummechtich
uncover	abdekka
under	unnah/unnich
understand	fashtay
understanding (n)	fashtand
undertake	unnah-nemma
undisciplined	ungland
undisturbed	blohk-frei
undoubtedly	gevislich
unexpected	unfahoft
unfamiliar	fremd
unfruitful	unfruchtboah
ungodliness	ungetlichkeit
ungodly	ungetlich
unholy	ungeishtlich
unintelligent	dumm
unity	aynichkeit
unknown	unbekand
unlearned	ungland
unleavened	unksavvaht
unmarried	leddich
unnecessary	unaydich
unrest	unroo
unrighteous	ungerecht/-ich
unrighteousness	ungerechtichkeit
unshrunken	unkshrunka
unstable	unshtandhaftich
untalented	unkshikt
unthankful	undankboah

until	biss
untruth	unvoahret
unwilling	unvillich
up from below	ruff
up in the air	hay
up there	drovva
uppermost	evvahsht
upset, capsize	umshmeisa
upside down	unnahs-evvahsht
upstairs	shpeichah
upward	nuff
us	uns
use	yoosa
use caution	yo
use sparingly	shpoahra

V

various	unnahshidlich
vault (n)	sayf
very	heslich/oahrich
vessel for carrying liquid	kann
vile	greislich
vinegar	essich
vineyard	drauva-feld/-goahra/vei-goahra
viscous substance	shmiah
visit (v)	psucha
visitor, company	psuch
visitors, company	psuch-leit
voice (n)	shtimm
volition	villa
voluntarily	frei-villich
vomit (n)	kotz

vomit (v)	kotza
voracious	fafressa
vote (v)	rohda
vow (v)	shveahra

W

wages	lohn
wagon, large	vauwa
wail (v)	yammahra
wait (v)	voahra
walk (v)	lawfa
walk of life	layves-lawf
wall	mavvah/vand
want	vella
war (n)	greek
warm (adj)	voahm
warm (v)	veahma
warn	favanna/vanna
warning	vanning
was	voah
was (past perfect tense)	gvest
wash (v)	vesha
washbowl	vesh-shissel
watch (n)	vatsh
watch (v)	vatsha
water (n)	vassah
water hole	vassah-loch
wave of water	vell
way	vayk
we	miah
weak	matt/shvach
weakness	shvachheit

wear	veahra
wear out	ausveahra
weather	veddah
wedding	hochtzich
wedding party	hochtzich-leit
weeds	veetz
week	voch
weep	heila/veina
weight	gvicht
weighty	vichtich
well (n)	brunna
well (preface to a remark)	vell
were	voahra
west	vest
wet (adj)	nass
whale	valfish
what	vass
whatever	vass-evvah
wheat	vaytza
when	vann
whenever	vann-evvah
where	vo
wherefore, why	vohheah
wherever	vo'evvah
whether	eb
which (relative pronoun)	es
which one	vels
while	veil
while, a little	veil
whip (n)	fitz
whisper (v)	pishpahra
whistle (n)	peif

whistler	peifah
white	veis
whitewash	veisla
who	veah
who (relative pronoun)	es
whoever	veah-evvah
wholesome	heilsam
whom	vemm
whoremonger	huahrah
whose	vemm sei
why	favass/vohheah
why (preface to a remark)	vei
wick	veecha
wicked	veesht
wickedly	veeshtahlich
widow	vitt-fraw/vitt-veib
wide	brayt
width	brayding
wife	fraw
wild	vild
wilderness	vildahnis
will, shall	zayl
willing	villich
willingly	villichlich
wilt	favelka
wilted (adj)	velk
win (v)	beeda
wind (n)	vind
window	fenshtah
windstorm	vind-shtoahm
wine	vei
wine drinker	vei-saufah

winepress	vei-press
wine vat	vei-drohk
wineskin	vei-sakk
wing	flikkel
winnowing fork	dresha-shaufel
winter	vindah
wisdom	veisheit
wish (v)	vinsha/vodda
with	mitt
with each other	mitt-nannah
with them	midna/mitt'na
wither (v)	dadda/fadadda
without	unni
without understanding	unfashtendlich
witness (n)	zeiya/zeiyah
witness (v)	zeiya
woe	vay
wolf	volf
woman	fraw/veib
womb	muddah's-leib
won	gvunna
wonder (v)	vunnahra
wood	hols
wooden	holsich
wool	vull
word	vatt
word of blasphemy	leshtah-vatt
work (n)	eahvet/verk
work (v)	shaffa
work out	ausshaffa
worker	shaffah
worker of evil	eevil-shaffah

works, meritorious	fadeensht
world	veld
worldly	veldlich
worm (n)	voahm
worm (v)	veahma
worried (adj)	bang
worry (n)	seik
worship (of idols)	abgeddah-deensht
worship (v)	deena/ohbayda
worship service	Gottes-deensht
worshipper of idols	abgott-deenah
worth	veaht
worthwhile	diveaht/veahtfollich
worthy	veahtfol
would	dayt/dayda
would be	veah/veahra
would be able	kent/kenda
would have	hett/hedda
would have to	mist/mista
would know	vist/vista
would need	breicht/breichta
would want	vett/vedda
wrap (v)	vikla
wrinkle (n)	runsel
write	shreiva
write off	abshreiva
wrong (adj)	letz
wrong (v)	faletza

Y

yard, unit of measure	yoaht
year	yoah

yell (v)	greisha
yellow	gayl
yes	yau
yes (contradicts a negative statement)	yo
yesterday	geshtah
yet	alsnoch/noch
yoke (n)	yoch
you	dich, du
you (plural)	diah/eich
young	yung
your	dei/deim/deina/deinra
your (plural)	eiyah/eiyahm
yours	dein

Z

zeal	eahnsht